Mattress Lux

Discover How to Redefine Your Sleep

Matt Wolf

Published by Freiling Agency, LLC.

P.O. Box 1264
Warrenton, VA 20188

www.FreilingAgency.com

PB ISBN: 978-1-963701-62-3
E-book ISBN: 978-1-963701-63-0

Contents

Introduction

A mattress isn't just where you sleep—
it's where rest begins. When your body is sustained,
your mind can finally let go, and that's where true rest—
and true peace—takes root.

—Matt Wolf

PEOPLE OFTEN ASK me, "Matt, why are you so obsessed with sleep?" It's a fair question. I've been helping people make better sleep decisions for over 20 years. But my passion for sleep didn't come from textbooks or scientific studies—though I've read plenty of those. It came from personal experience. A hard-earned, sometimes painful, but always eye-opening experience.

Long before I ever stepped foot in a mattress store, I was chasing a completely different dream. I was in the entertainment business in Hollywood, running full speed with stars in my eyes and big dreams in my back pocket. I thought I was on top of the world. But somewhere along the way, I lost some perspective. I started living for the spotlight, the thrill, and the next big rush. Everything felt exciting, but I was having too much fun to realize I was drifting off course. My life was loud, fast, and full of distractions—but it wasn't full of meaning.

That's when a friend stepped in and offered me something I didn't even know I needed: a lifeline. He walked with me, listened to me, and, little by little, pointed me toward something greater than myself. Through that friendship, I found faith—real faith. Not just religion or routine but a relationship with God that started to reshape everything in my life. And with that faith came something I hadn't felt in years: peace. Not the kind of peace that comes from a weekend getaway or a good night's sleep—but deep, soul-level peace. The kind that quiets your heart clears your mind, and reminds you who you really are.

Frankly, I didn't realize how badly I needed rest until I actually experienced it. I was so used to running 24/7 that I had forgotten what stillness felt like. I had no peace, no rhythm, no real rest in my life. But when I surrendered and let God lead the way, I began to learn what it meant to be still. I started to sleep again—not just physically, but spiritually and emotionally. And that changed everything.

At the time, I was working as a salesperson at a local mattress store. Not exactly the stage I imagined I'd be on—but it was the perfect place for a new beginning. I started listening to people. I mean really listening. And I realized something powerful: sleep was a pain point for almost everyone. People were stressed, restless, anxious, and exhausted—not just physically but mentally and emotionally too.

That's when it started to hit me. If I could help people find better sleep, maybe I could help them with more than just "comfort" – but rest. And that became my mission. From that day forward, I committed myself to helping people rest better—not just with the right mattress or pillow, but with the right mindset, the right habits, and the right priorities.

Over the past two decades, I've worked with some of the largest and most respected mattress manufacturers in America, helping design and refine products that millions of people sleep on every night. I've consulted on everything from comfort layers to support systems, always with one goal in mind: helping people sleep better. I've traveled coast to coast, training retail teams, advising sleep consultants and working one-on-one with customers to solve their biggest sleep challenges. From factory floors to bedroom showrooms, I've seen it all— and I've learned what truly works. My experience has given me a deep understanding and mission of how the right mattress can radically improve not just sleep but quality of life.

This book is part of that mission. Because sleep is not just comfort; it's about healing, renewal, clarity, and peace. And I'm here to help you find it.

The Sleep Crisis

Over the years, I've seen firsthand just how many people are walking around in a constant state of exhaustion. I can't tell you how often someone walks into a mattress store, rubs their eyes, and says, "I just need to sleep better." They're tossing and turning every night, hitting the snooze button every morning, and reaching for coffee like it's a life raft. And here's the scary part:

most people are so used to feeling tired that they think it's normal. It's not. It's just common.

The numbers back this up. According to the CDC, about 1 in 3 adults in the United States report not getting enough sleep regularly. That's more than 100 million people who are chronically sleep-deprived. Another National Sleep Foundation study found that 45% of Americans say poor or insufficient sleep affects their daily activities at least weekly. That's nearly half the country operating at a fraction of their potential—and accepting it as just the way life is.

But it doesn't have to be that way. Sleep is not a luxury. It's not something you "catch up on" later. It's foundational to every part of your health—your brain, your body, your mood, your relationships, your decision-making, and yes, even your dreams. When you're well-rested, everything changes. You think clearer, you feel better, you appear stronger. That's what I want for you. Not just more hours in bed—but real, restorative, life-giving sleep that fuels the best version of you.

How Do You Know If You're Really Rested?

Most people don't actually know what being well-rested feels like—because they haven't experienced it in years. You might be functioning, sure. You're going to work, running errands, meeting deadlines. But deep down, you're probably running on fumes. One of the biggest red flags? Needing caffeine to "get going" every morning or sugar to push through the afternoon. Another one? Getting 7 or 8 hours of sleep and still waking up feeling like you got hit by a truck.

True rest shows up in more than just how long you sleep—it shows up in how you feel. Are you waking up refreshed or groggy? Are you clear-headed or foggy? Do you crash by 3 p.m. or stay mentally sharp all day? Are your emotions stable, or are you easily frustrated, anxious, or down? If you're always tired, always dragging, or just "meh" all the time, your body is waving a big red flag. And most of us ignore it.

Here's a simple truth: your body is not designed to be in fight-or-flight mode 24/7. Rest is not just about recharging your phone overnight—it's about recharging *you*. When you're truly rested, you don't just survive— you thrive. You're present, joyful, focused, and energized. And if that doesn't sound like your current reality, don't worry. This book is here to help you get there.

Fix Your Bed, Fix Your Sleep

Now, let me be clear—I'm not a doctor. I'm not here to diagnose sleep disorders or get into all the medical reasons people struggle with sleep. There are specialists for that, and if you suspect something more serious like sleep apnea or chronic insomnia, by all means, talk to your doctor. What I *am* here to do is focus on the part of sleep that often gets overlooked: your actual sleep environment. And,d more specifically, your mattress.

In my 20+ years of working with people from every background imaginable, one truth keeps rising to the surface: your mattress plays a huge role in the quality of your sleep. In fact, it may be the most important factor. You can do everything else right—stick to a bedtime routine, cut out screens before bed, sip herbal tea, even meditate—but if your mattress is uncomfortable, unsupportive, or just plain worn out, your body won't relax, and your sleep will suffer. That's just the reality.

But here's the other side of that coin: even the most advanced, top-rated mattress in the world won't help if it's not right for *you*. What feels like heaven for one person might feel like a rock for another. And even if you do have the perfect mattress for your body, if you ignore the things you *do* during the day—stress, caffeine, screen time, poor habits—you'll still struggle to fall asleep and stay asleep. Deep, restorative sleep requires both the right foundation beneath you and the right behaviors around you.

That's where I come in. My passion is helping people make better sleep decisions—starting with the surface you sleep on. Over the years, I've helped thousands of people find the right mattress for their bodies, their budget, and their lifestyle. I've seen lives transformed just by getting people on the right bed. Because when your body is properly supported, and your sleep environment is dialed in, your brain can relax, your muscles can recover, and your entire system can reset. It's not magic. It's just what happens when you sleep the way you were designed to.

Time to zzzzzzzz!

So what do we do now? Simple—we start where you sleep. This book is going to help you rethink your relationship with rest. We'll talk about what's stealing your sleep, what you can do to get it back, and how to create a sleep environment that works for you, not against you. You don't need to be a sleep scientist to get better sleep—you just need the right tools, the right setup, and a little bit of guidance from someone who's been helping people sleep better for decades.

We'll break down the basics of mattress selection, dive into sleep habits that make a difference, and explore how rest impacts your body, mind, mood, and relationships. You might be surprised how much changes when you start sleeping better. Better decisions. Better focus. More patience. More joy. That's not just good sleep—that's a better life.

Your mattress isn't just furniture—it's the foundation of your rest. Think about it: you spend a third of your life lying. That's more time than you'll spend in your car, at your desk, or on your sofa combined. If your mattress isn't properly supporting your spine, relieving pressure points, and keeping your body aligned, your muscles will stay tense all night. You'll toss, turn, wake up stiff, and never quite hit those deep, restorative stages of sleep your body needs. A quality mattress removes those barriers. It cradles your body in all the right places so you can relax fully, breathe deeply, and stay asleep longer.

That's not hype—it's how your body was designed to function. And when your bed works with you instead of against you, everything changes.

Finding True Rest

So, if you're tired of being tired, you're in the right place. My goal is to help you find the kind of rest that restores your body and your soul. Because when you finally experience true rest, you'll never settle for anything less again. At the end of the day, better sleep isn't just about comfort—it's about rest and restoration.

How do I know?

I told you how my life changed in Hollywood. Even today, I'm still a Christian. That's at the center of who I am, and it deeply shapes the way I see rest, peace, and purpose. Now, if that's not your story, that's totally okay. You're still welcome here, and I believe this book will help you in powerful, practical ways no matter what you believe. But for me, faith was the turning point. When my life was spinning out of control, it was God who brought me back to the center. It was through my faith that I discovered a kind of peace that went beyond my circumstances—a peace that grounded me, healed me, and gave me a fresh start.

That peace didn't come overnight. It came slowly, through surrender and stillness. Through learning to let go and trust. And it's that same peace that has fueled my desire to help others—because I know what it's like to live without it. I know what it's like to be restless on the inside, even when everything on the outside looks fine. That's why this journey matters so much to me.

So yes, we're going to talk about sleep. We're going to talk about mattresses, routines, environments, and habits. But my hope is that somewhere along the way, you'll also discover something deeper. Something even richer! That you'll begin to experience rest not just in your body— but in your soul. Because real rest goes far beyond the mattress, and when you find it, it changes everything!

1

My Sleep Story

SO, MY SLEEP story didn't end when I left Los Angeles. In many ways, it was just beginning.

After walking away from the fast-paced chaos of the entertainment world, I found myself back in familiar territory: a mattress store. It wasn't glamorous. It wasn't flashy. But it felt... honest. Grounded. Real. I knew the ropes from my earlier experience, and it didn't take long for me to find a rhythm again—connecting with customers, asking the right questions, and helping people navigate the surprisingly complex world of mattresses. But this time, I saw it differently. I wasn't just selling beds—I was helping people rest. And I was starting to think more deeply about what that really meant.

One afternoon, a young man walked into the store holding his right shoulder, wincing slightly with every step. His face was tight with pain, and you could tell this wasn't just a rough night's sleep—this had been building for a while.

"Hey man," he said, trying to smile. "I'm looking for a new mattress. My shoulder's been killing me. I can't sleep."

I nodded. "Is it your right side?"

"Yeah," he said, surprised. "How'd you know?"

"It's in the way you're holding your arm," I said. "Let me ask—are you a side sleeper?"

"Always," he replied. "Can't sleep any other way."

I smiled and motioned him over to a specific mattress. "You need pressure relief. Something that cradles your shoulder instead of jamming it all night. Try this one."

He laid down, slowly, cautiously—and then his eyes widened.

"Whoa… this feels amazing," he said, almost in disbelief. "Like, instantly better."

He bought the mattress that day. A week later, he called me.

"Matt, I had to call and say thank you," he said. "My shoulder already feels better. I've actually been sleeping through the night. I can't believe it."

And right then, I felt it. That click. That moment of clarity. It was like something inside me lit up. *This is it*, I thought. *This is what I was made to do.* Not just to sell mattresses. Not just to talk about sleep. But to help people heal. To help them rest. To be a guide—someone who shows up when life feels off track and offers a path back to peace, starting with something as simple and powerful as a good night's sleep.

That call was my epiphany moment. That's when everything shifted. That's when my career became a calling.

So I went to work for some of the country's biggest and most respected mattress designers and manufacturers—names you'd instantly recognize, the giants of the industry. It was like stepping behind the curtain and seeing how the magic was made. I dove in headfirst, eager to learn every detail: the science of sleep, the engineering behind support systems, the chemistry of foams and fabrics, and the biomechanics of spinal alignment. I asked questions, toured factories, tested prototypes, and sat in on meetings with product developers who'd been in the game for decades. I soaked it all in. I wasn't just interested—I was obsessed.

I wanted to understand *why* certain mattresses helped people sleep better and why others—no matter how expensive—left them sore, tired, and frustrated. I wanted to crack the code, to figure out how comfort and support could be perfectly balanced for different body types, sleep styles, and health conditions. I studied airflow, motion isolation, cooling technologies, pressure mapping—you name it. I became a student of sleep.

Soon, I wasn't just learning—I was teaching. I started training retail teams nationwide, traveling from coast to coast, helping thousands of sleep consultants, store managers, and salespeople understand the connection between sleep science and mattress design. I was living out of hotels, hopping on planes, and logging long hours—but I loved it. Because everywhere I went, I saw the same thing. People were desperate for better sleep, and they had no idea where to start. I got to be their guide. And I never took that lightly.

A New Life

This was my life for many years—traveling, teaching, learning, and living out my mission to help people sleep better. And during that time, life kept moving forward. I got married to the love of my life, and together we started a family. Those were beautiful, busy years—full of growth, joy, diapers, dinner-time chaos, and deep gratitude. I absolutely loved my work, but as my kids grew, I started to feel a pull. I didn't want to be the dad who was always on the road, always catching flights and missing bedtimes. I wanted to be present not just for the big moments—but for the small, quiet, everyday ones that matter most.

My wife and I started talking about what that might look like. We prayed about it. A lot. And over time, the answer became clear. It was time to stop traveling so much. It was time to plant roots, build something close to home, and invest more deeply in both my family and my community. So, after years of working with major brands and flying all over the country, we made the leap. We settled in the Atlanta area and took a huge step of faith: I decided to open my own mattress stores.

It wasn't an easy decision. Starting a business is always risky—and walking away from a successful career in training and consulting felt like a big gamble. But deep down, I was inspired. I wanted to take everything I had learned—the science, the experience, the passion—and bring it directly to customers in a way that felt different.

Personal. Trustworthy. Real. I didn't want to just sell mattresses; I wanted to create a space where people could come in tired and overwhelmed... and leave with hope, confidence, and the promise of a better night's sleep. That was the dream. And by God's grace, it became a reality. Mattress Lux was born!

Today, nothing means more to me than when a customer comes back and says, "Matt, I'm sleeping better—and I feel like a different person." Those moments never get old. I've had people tell me their back pain is gone, their energy is up, their mood is better, and their marriage feels stronger because they're finally sleeping through the night. And every time I hear that, it reminds me why I do this. It's not just about selling a product—it's about changing lives.

Rest isn't a luxury; it's a basic need. And when someone finds it after years of struggle, you can see it in their face. They walk a little lighter. They smile more. That transformation is the most rewarding part of my job.

I've had people hug me. I've had people tear up. I've had customers send friends and family my way because they finally felt seen and helped. Those stories stick with me. They remind me that sleep isn't just a physical thing—it's emotional, spiritual, and relational. When you're rested, you show up differently in the world. You become more present, more patient, more fully yourself. And knowing I got to play even a small part in that journey? That's the kind of work I'll never take for granted.

Here's What Happens When You Don't Sleep Well

Let me be upfront about something important: I'm not a medical doctor, and I'm not a licensed medical professional. I can't diagnose sleep disorders, prescribe treatments, or tell you if your sleep issues are part of a larger health condition. That's not my role—and I respect the professionals trained to do that kind of work. So if you're dealing with chronic sleep problems, waking up gasping for air, struggling with anxiety or depression, or if something just feels off, please don't ignore it. Talk to your doctor. There are incredible resources and experts who can help.

That said, after more than two decades in the sleep industry, I've seen patterns—thousands of them. I've spent years talking with people about their sleep issues, their frustrations, their pain, and what finally helped them rest. I've listened, I've studied, and I've helped people troubleshoot their sleep one mattress, one routine, one small decision at a time. I may not wear a white coat, but I've learned something about what keeps people up at night—and what it looks like when you don't get a good night's sleep.

Mental Fog and Poor Focus

Your brain pays the price when you don't get enough quality sleep. Your ability to focus, make decisions, and think clearly takes a major hit. Even simple tasks feel overwhelming. Sleep deprivation slows down your reaction time and clouds your thinking—kind of like trying to drive through heavy fog. Over time, this mental fatigue can seriously affect your productivity, memory, and performance at work or school.

Weight Gain and Cravings

Lack of sleep messes with the hormones that regulate hunger—ghrelin and leptin. When you're sleep-deprived, your body craves more calories, especially sugar and carbs. That's why it's so easy to overeat when you're tired. Plus, your metabolism slows, making it harder to burn those extra calories. Poor sleep can quietly sabotage your weight loss goals and lead to unwanted weight gain.

Weakened Immune System

Your body does most of its healing while you sleep. So when you're not getting enough rest, your immune system can't function properly. That means you're more likely to catch colds viruses, and even take longer to recover from illnesses. Chronic sleep deprivation can leave your body constantly playing defense, making it harder to stay healthy and bounce back.

Increased Risk of Heart Disease

Sleep is critical for heart health. During deep sleep, your heart rate and blood pressure drop, giving your cardiovascular system a much-needed break. But without proper rest, those numbers stay elevated, putting more strain on your heart. Long-term sleep deprivation has been linked to a higher risk of hypertension, heart attack, and stroke.

Emotional Instability

Ever notice how everything feels heavier after a bad night's sleep? You're more irritable more anxious, and your ability to manage stress shrinks. That's because sleep is essential for emotional regulation. Without it, the brain's emotional center—the amygdala—goes into overdrive while the rational part of your brain struggles to keep up. Over time, poor sleep can contribute to mood swings, depression, and burnout.

If any of these things sound familiar—mental fog, weight gain, getting sick more often, high stress, or just feeling emotionally off—you're not alone. These are all warning signs that your body and mind are empty. The good news? You don't have to stay stuck in that cycle. Sleep is one of the most powerful forms of self-care you can give yourself; even small changes can lead to big improvements. If you're tired of being tired, this book is for you. Let's start rebuilding your rest—one step at a time.

In the next chapter, we'll explore sleep and what it means to get a good night's sleep. We'll start by examining the four stages of sleep and why they are each so important.

2

Behind the Scenes of Sleep

MOST PEOPLE THINK of sleep as a simple on-off switch—you're either awake or asleep. But the truth is, sleep is much more complex and fascinating than that. Your body cycles through several distinct stages of sleep each night, and each one plays a unique role in helping you feel rested, restored, and ready for a new day. Understanding these stages can give you powerful insight into why some nights leave you feeling refreshed—and others leave you groggy, no matter how many hours you clocked. In this chapter, we'll break down the stages of sleep, what happens in each one, and why they all matter more than you might think.

But first, you might be asking, "What do the stages of sleep have to do with your mattress?" A lot, actually. Your body needs to stay comfortable and supported to move through the full sleep cycle—especially into the deeper, more restorative stages like deep sleep and REM. If your mattress causes pressure points, poor alignment, or constant tossing and turning, it can disrupt those critical transitions between stages. You might fall asleep, but your sleep will be shallow and fragmented. The right mattress helps keep your body relaxed and still, allowing your brain to move smoothly through the natural rhythms of the night. In short, a good mattress doesn't just help you fall asleep—it helps you stay and sleep well.

Now, let's take a closer look at what your body and brain are actually doing while you're sleeping. Sleep isn't one long, uniform state—it's a cycle of four distinct stages, each with its own unique purpose. These stages work together like a well-choreographed routine, repeatedly throughout the night. The better your body can move through each stage, the more refreshed, focused, and energized you'll feel the next day. So let's break it down—stage by stage—so you can understand exactly what's happening while you rest.

Stage 1: Light Sleep – The Transition Phase

The first stage of sleep is short light, and it acts as the bridge between wakefulness and rest. This is when your brain transitions from full alertness to slower brain wave activity. Your muscles begin to relax, your heartbeat slows, and your body temperature drops. Stage 1 only lasts a few minutes—usually 5 to 10—and is the easiest to wake up from. You may experience slight muscle twitches, sudden jerks, or even that falling sensation that jolts you awake. This is your body beginning its descent into deeper rest.

Stage 1 might not feel like much, but it's an important part of the sleep process. It sets the tone for the night. If you're constantly being disturbed—by a loud environment, an uncomfortable mattress, or a racing mind—you may keep cycling in and out of this light sleep stage and never get the deep rest you need. That's why having a supportive and comfortable sleep setup is so important. You need a mattress that invites your body to relax and stay relaxed so you can successfully transition into deeper stages of sleep.

Stage 2: Deper Light Sleep – Body Maintenance Begins

Stage 2 is still considered light sleep, but your body begins to shut down more noticeably here. Brain wave activity slows further with occasional bursts of electrical activity called *sleep spindles*, which are thought to play a role in memory consolidation and learning. Your heart rate keeps dropping, your muscles relax even more, and your eye movements stop. This stage typically makes up about 50% of your total sleep each night.

This is where your body begins the real work of physical recovery—regulating hormones, adjusting blood pressure, and stabilizing internal systems. If your mattress doesn't support proper spinal alignment or if it causes pressure points, your body might constantly shift and disrupt this crucial stage. A good mattress helps maintain a neutral posture, minimizing movement and giving your nervous system a calm environment to do its job without interruption. This is where sleep begins to *restore* you, not just *rest* you.

Stage 3: Deep Sleep – The Healing Zone

Stage 3 is what we often call deep sleep or slow-wave sleep. This is the most restorative sleep stage for your body. Your brain waves slow down dramatically, your breathing becomes more rhythmic, and your muscles are fully relaxed. It's during this stage that your body repairs tissue, builds muscle, strengthens the immune system, and releases growth hormone. Deep sleep is absolutely essential for physical health and recovery.

When people say they wake up sore, stiff, or just as tired as when they went to bed, it's often because they didn't get enough time at this stage. A poor mattress can cause tossing and turning that pulls your body out of deep sleep before it's finished doing its job. You want a bed that supports your pressure points, keeps you still, and allows your muscles to fully let go. That's the difference between sleep that just passes time—and sleep that actually *heals* you.

Stage 4: REM Sleep – The Brain's Turn to Recharge

The final sleep stage is REM, which stands for Rapid Eye Movement. This is when your brain becomes highly active again, nearly mimicking the activity levels of wakefulness. It's the stage where most of your vivid dreams occur. REM plays a crucial role in memory processing, emotional regulation, creativity, and learning. Your breathing becomes irregular, your heart rate rises, and your eyes move rapidly under your eyelids—yet your muscles remain temporarily paralyzed to prevent you from acting out your dreams.

REM sleep is especially important for mental and emotional health. If you're consistently missing REM— due to stress, alcohol, medications, or a disrupted sleep environment—you may notice mood swings, difficulty concentrating, and higher anxiety levels. This is why your mattress still matters even in the dreaming phase. If you're frequently waking up from discomfort, over-heating, or poor movement isolation, your brain is being pulled away from the work it needs to do. A well-designed sleep surface creates the conditions your brain needs to complete its nightly recharge.

What Happens When You Skip Sleep Stages

When you don't consistently reach Stage 1 and Stage 2, your sleep becomes fragmented, and your body struggles to make the transition from wakefulness to rest. You may fall asleep but quickly wake up again, leading to that frustrating "tired but wired" feeling. Without enough time in these lighter stages, your body never fully winds down, your heart rate stays elevated, and your nervous system doesn't shift into recovery mode. This disruption often happens when your sleep environment is uncomfortable—think of a mattress that's too firm, too soft, or just plain worn out. Your body can't relax if it's constantly shifting to find relief.

Missing out on Stage 3, or deep sleep, robs your body of the time it needs to heal, repair, and restore itself. This is the stage where your immune system is strengthened, muscle and tissue are rebuilt, and energy is replenished for the next day. Without it, you may wake up feeling stiff, sore, or exhausted, even after eight hours in bed. Over time, the lack of deep sleep can lead to chronic fatigue, weakened immunity, and even increase your risk for long-term health issues like heart disease and diabetes. Your body desperately needs this stage—but it can't get there if your mattress isn't supporting your pressure points and keeping you comfortably still.

Skipping REM sleep also has a direct impact on your brain and emotional health. Without REM, your memory suffers, your ability to concentrate decreases, and your mood can spiral. You might feel forgetful, anxious, overly emotional, or just "off." REM is when your brain processes everything it learned that day, clears out the mental clutter, and resets for the next. If your sleep is regularly interrupted—say, from tossing and turning on a poor mattress—you may be cutting off REM before it can do its job. Over time, this can contribute to burnout, mental fog, and even depression. That's why protecting your REM sleep is just as vital as deep sleep—and why your mattress matters more than most people realize.

How To Stay In Your Sleep Stages Longer

So if you find yourself waking frequently or struggling to fall asleep in the first place, chances are you're not getting enough of the lighter stages—**Stages 1 and 2**. These are critical transition points that prepare your body and brain for deeper sleep. To support these stages, focus on creating a calming pre-bed routine: dim the lights, turn off screens an hour before bed, and avoid caffeine in the afternoon. Make sure your bedroom feels like a sanctuary—cool, quiet, and clutter-free. And,d of course, make sure your mattress helps you ease into relaxation, not resist it. If you're tossing and turning within the first hour of sleep, your mattress might be too firm or not conforming to your body properly.

If you wake up feeling physically sore or exhausted— even after a full night in bed—you may be missing out on **deep sleep** (Stage 3). This could be a result of frequent body movement or discomfort throughout the night. Pressure-relieving mattresses, like those with memory foam or zoned support, can help your muscles fully relax and stay still so your body can enter deep sleep. Creating a consistent bedtime and wake time also helps your body enter this stage more efficiently. If you find yourself getting sick often or feeling physically run down, it's a good sign your body isn't getting the deep, healing rest it needs.

When it comes to **REM sleep**, the clues are mostly mental and emotional. Are you moody, forgetful, or unable to concentrate? Do you wake up feeling emotionally drained or anxious? These may be signs your brain isn't spending enough time in REM. To improve REM sleep, avoid alcohol and heavy meals close to bedtime— both can disrupt this stage. Stress is another major REM disruptor, so wind down your mind at night with calming rituals like journaling, reading, or prayer. And remember, your mattress still plays a part here. Frequent awakenings—even small ones you don't remember—can pull you out of REM and prevent your brain from doing its cleanup work. Protect your sleep environment, and you protect your peace.

Is Your Sleep Off-Track?

Here's a simple "Is Your Sleep Off Track?" Quiz to help you identify which stage(s) of sleep you might be missing. Remember, I'm not a doctor. You might want to consult your physician if you're concerned about your sleep and health.

Falling Asleep and Staying Asleep (Stages 1 and 2):

- ☐ It takes me more than 30 minutes to fall asleep most nights.
- ☐ I wake up frequently throughout the night.
- ☐ I feel alert or "wired" even when I'm tired.

☐ My mind races the minute my head hits the pillow.

☐ I dread bedtime because I know I'll struggle to fall asleep.

If you checked two or more of these, you may be stuck in the lighter stages of sleep and struggling to transition into deeper rest.

Physical Recovery (Stage 3 – Deep Sleep):

☐ I wake up feeling sore, stiff, or physically tired.
☐ I sleep "enough" hours but still feel drained.
☐ I get sick often or take a long time to recover.
☐ I toss and turn to get comfortable.
☐ I often wake up sweaty or too hot/cold.

If you checked two or more of these, your body may not be getting the deep sleep it needs for physical healing and recovery.

Mental and Emotional Recharge (Stage 4 – REM Sleep):

☐ I have trouble concentrating or feel mentally foggy.
☐ My memory isn't what it used to be.
☐ I'm more emotional, irritable, or anxious lately.
☐ I rarely remember my dreams.
☐ I wake up feeling emotionally exhausted.

If you checked two or more of these, you may not be reaching or staying in REM sleep long enough for your brain to recharge.

What Your Results Mean:

If you checked boxes across all three categories, don't worry—you're not alone. Most people are missing out on at least one stage of quality sleep. The good news is that the rest of this book is designed to help you identify what's causing the disruption and guide you step-by-step toward better rest.

3

Breaking the Sleep Cycle

AS WE SAW above, the true key to a great night's sleep is getting enough deep sleep and REM sleep through the *completion* of full sleep cycles. In a perfect world, we would complete five to six sleep cycles every night—moving smoothly from light sleep into deep sleep, into REM, and back again—waking up fully restored, focused, energized, and firing on all cylinders. But we don't live in a perfect world. We live in a world of interruptions, stress, technology, and physical discomfort. All of these things—and more—can hinder us from completing our sleep cycles and, ultimately, from getting the kind of deep rest we were made for.

Sleep Deprivation

Sleep disturbance often leads directly to sleep deprivation. And that's not just about how many hours you're in bed—it's about the *quality* of those hours. Deprivation comes from not getting enough sleep or not getting enough *good* sleep over an extended period of time.

And here's the tricky part: sleep deprivation doesn't always announce itself loudly. It's sneaky. The signs are often subtle, gradual, and easy to dismiss—until one day, you realize you've been living in a fog for weeks, maybe even years.

You may be sleep-deprived if you:

- Need an alarm clock in order to wake up on time
- Rely on the snooze button
- Have a hard time getting out of bed in the morning
- Feel sluggish in the afternoon
- Get sleepy in meetings, lectures, or warm rooms
- Get drowsy after heavy meals or when driving
- Need to nap to get through the day
- Fall asleep while watching TV or relaxing in the evening
- Feel the need to sleep in on weekends
- Fall asleep within five minutes of going to bed

These may seem like normal everyday things—but they're not. They're warning signs. They're your body's saying, "Hey, I'm running on empty here."

One of the most common and overlooked causes of sleep deprivation is frequent *nighttime awakenings*. You might think you're getting a full eight hours, but if you're being woken up during a sleep cycle—especially during deep sleep or REM—your brain and body never get the chance to complete the restorative work they're designed to do. Each time you're jolted awake, your body has to start the cycle over again. Even if you're not fully conscious of these wakeups, they fragment your sleep and reduce your time in the critical stages that fuel healing, memory, mood, and energy. The result? You wake up feeling groggy, irritable, and unrefreshed, even though you technically "slept" for a decent amount of time.

While some sleep disruptions are out of our control— crying babies, loud neighbors, or barking dogs—many *are* within our power to manage. Once you identify and address these hidden sleep stealers, you can dramatically improve your quality of rest. In the next section, we'll walk through the four most common, fixable disturbances that might sabotage your sleep—and, more importantly, what you can do to stop them. No,w let's dive into the four primary sleep disturbances.

Pressure Points: The Midnight Aches

One of the most common yet misunderstood causes of sleep disturbance is pressure points. These occur when certain parts of your body—usually your hips, shoulders, arms, or legs—bear too much weight against the mattress without enough cushioning or support. This pressure compresses the tiny capillaries in those areas, reducing blood flow. Ever woken up in the middle of the night with a numb arm, tingly fingers, or cold feet? That's your body responding to a circulation issue caused by pressure points. And more often than not, your *mattress* is the culprit.

Here's where it gets even more interesting: during deep sleep, your brain doesn't want to be disturbed. And during REM sleep, your voluntary muscles are essentially paralyzed to prevent you from acting out your dreams. But your brain is incredibly smart—and protective. It knows that if a limb loses circulation for too long, the cells in that area can begin to die. So what does it do? It *pulls you out* of deep or REM sleep just enough to make you move. This is why people toss and turn at night without ever fully waking up. Your brain is doing its job—it's saving your arm!

The bad news? Every time this happens, your sleep cycle gets interrupted. If your mattress isn't relieving pressure well, your brain will keep hitting the reset button on your sleep cycle, preventing you from ever reaching or completing the deep, restorative stages. That's why pressure-relieving foams—like memory foam or latex—can make such a massive difference. They contour to your body, distribute weight evenly, and reduce the need for your brain to intervene just to keep your blood flowing constantly.

Improper Support: Your Mis-aligned Spine

While pressure relief is all about comfort, support is all about structure—and both are absolutely essential for great sleep. Proper support in a mattress keeps your spine aligned while you rest. Many people don't realize that the spine isn't just a stack of bones—it's surrounded by dozens of large and small muscles that work constantly to keep your body upright, stable, and moving correctly throughout the day. But when you fall asleep—especially in deep sleep or REM—your body intentionally shuts down your larger muscle groups. Your muscles relax, and your body becomes still so your brain can do its nightly recovery work.

This means that during the deepest parts of your sleep, your mattress becomes fully responsible for keeping your spine in alignment. If your mattress isn't offering the right support—either because it's too soft, too firm, or has broken down over time—your spine starts to sag or twist slightly out of position. That's when your involuntary support muscles, which are much smaller than your larger back muscles, kick in to try and compensate. These little muscles work overtime to keep you aligned, but they can only do so much. And once they fatigue, your brain kicks into protective mode—pulling you out of deep or REM sleep to trigger a shift in position. Just like with pressure points, this constant shifting interrupts your sleep cycle, keeping you from getting the true rest your body needs.

When your mattress provides proper support, it allows those deep muscles to relax without stress or strain completely. Your body stays still, your spine stays aligned, and your brain gets the message that everything is okay—no need to wake up and shift. This is why support is as important as comfort. A well-supported spine equals deeper, more continuous sleep—and more completed sleep cycles.

Motion Transfer: The Toss and Turn Thief

One of the most common—and most frustrating—reasons people don't sleep well is because of their **sleep partner**. Whether it's a spouse, a child, or even a pet, sharing a bed means sharing movement—and that can be a real problem. "Motion transfer" happens when movement on one side of the bed is felt on the other side. So every time your partner rolls over, gets out of bed, flops back down, or even shifts position, that movement travels across the mattress and often wakes *you* up, too.

And here's the thing: even small movements matter. Every time your sleep is disrupted—especially when you're in deep sleep or REM—your brain is pulled out of its cycle. It may not seem like a big deal at the moment, but these tiny wake-ups add up. When you're repeatedly pulled out of deeper stages of sleep, your body can't complete the sleep cycles it needs to heal, recharge, and reset. That's why many people wake up feeling groggy and unrested, even after spending a full eight hours in bed. The quality of your sleep—not just the quantity—is what truly matters.

Thankfully, some mattresses are much better than others at reducing motion transfer. Materials like memory foam and natural latex can absorb movement, so it doesn't ripple across the bed like a wave. Certain hybrid mattresses, especially those with individually wrapped coils, also help reduce motion. If you or your partner are light sleepers—or if one of you tosses and turns a lot at night—it might be time to upgrade your mattress to one that helps you both sleep soundly. Because let's be honest: if one of you isn't sleeping well, *neither* of you really is.

Temperature Trouble: Night-time Climate Crisis

Here's something most people don't realize: while our bodies are great at regulating temperature during the day, things change dramatically at night—especially during REM sleep. As mammals, we're designed to maintain a consistent core temperature of around 98.6°F. But once we fall into REM sleep, the part of our brain responsible for temperature regulation goes offline. In a way, we temporarily become like reptiles—completely dependent on our external environment to stay warm or cool. If our environment isn't just right, our brain will pull us *out* of that critical sleep stage to adjust. And that, over time, leads to broken sleep cycles and serious fatigue.

Ever notice how you toss the covers off, then pull them back on again a few hours later? That's your body trying to manage its own temperature without the usual tools it has during the day. Maybe you've woken up in a sweat or with freezing feet, even though the thermostat hasn't changed. That's not just uncomfortable—it's disruptive. Each time your body gets too hot or too cold, your brain has to make a decision: stay in deep sleep or wake you up just enough to fix the problem. And guess what? Your brain almost always chooses to wake you—because survival trumps sleep.

The good news is that your mattress can play a huge role in keeping your temperature stable through the night. Your mattress's materials and design can trap heat or help you regulate it naturally. Here are a few ways modern mattresses help with temperature control:

1. **Breathable Fibers in the Cover**
   Covers made with breathable materials improve airflow and help prevent heat from getting trapped between your body and the mattress surface.

2. **Natural Fibers**
   Natural materials like cotton and wool wick away moisture and help your body stay cooler in the summer and warmer in the winter—making your sleep environment feel more balanced year-round.

3. **Gel-Infused Foam**
   Gel has the unique ability to absorb and disperse excess heat. When used properly in a mattress, it draws heat away from your body and keeps the sleeping surface cooler.

4. **Phase Change Material (PCM)**
   This high-tech material acts like a thermostat for your bed. It absorbs excess heat when you're too warm and releases it back when you get too cold—helping maintain a consistent, comfortable temperature all night long.

Choosing a mattress that actively helps regulate your temperature isn't just about comfort—it's about protecting your sleep cycles. And when your body stays in balance, your sleep gets deeper, your brain stays quieter, and you wake up feeling more rested than you have in years. We'll get into this more later in this book. But for now, I want you to better understand how central your mattress is for a good night's sleep.

The Secret to Fewer Sleep Disturbances

Here's the truth most people overlook: your mattress might be the biggest factor affecting your sleep. Yes, your stress level, screen time, and daily habits matter—but if you're lying on a surface that's uncomfortable, unsupportive, too hot, or constantly moving, your body never gets a chance to fully relax. Night after night, those disruptions add up. And no matter how early you go to bed or how many hours you log, poor sleep will still follow you into the next day.

Your mattress either works with your body—or against it. A bad mattress can create pressure points, force your spine out of alignment, shake you awake with every movement from your partner, or trap heat and make you sweat through the night. And when your body can't settle into deep or REM sleep, you're stuck in a constant cycle of light, restless sleep that leaves you feeling tired and frustrated. On the flip side, the right mattress helps your body stay still, your spine stays straight, and your temperature stays balanced. It keeps your brain calm and your body at peace. It literally sets the stage for better sleep—and a better life.

That's why your mattress isn't just a piece of furniture—it's a critical tool for your health, energy, and emotional well-being. So now that we've talked about the problems, it's time to dive into the solution. In the next chapter, we'll explore exactly how to choose the right mattress for you—based on your sleep style, body type, comfort preferences, and real-life needs. Let's take everything we've learned and put it into action. Your best sleep is closer than you think.

4

One Size Doesn't Fit All: Finding the Right Mattress for You

ONE DAY, A woman named Karen walked into the store with confidence in her step and a printout in her hand. She did her research, she told me. She'd read all the articles and canned all the reviews, and she was sure of what she needed.

"I want a firm mattress," she said, placing the paper on the counter like it was a prescription. "Everyone online says firm is best for your back."

I smiled. "Firm can be great—for the right person," I said. "Mind if I ask how you usually sleep?"

"On my side," she replied quickly. "Kind of curled up."

That's when I gently tapped the brakes.

"Okay, that's helpful. So here's the thing—if you're a side sleeper and you go too firm, you might end up with sore shoulders and hips. You need pressure relief in those areas. If your mattress pushes *back* too hard, it can cut off circulation and cause discomfort, which means your brain will keep waking you up to shift."

She blinked. "I had no idea. I just assumed firmer meant better quality."

And there it was—the moment of realization. The same one I've seen hundreds of times. People walk into mattress stores every day asking, *"What's the best mattress?"* But that's the wrong question. The right question is, *"What's the best mattress for me?"*

I looked at Karen and smiled. "Let's forget the reviews for a second. Let's listen to your body. How do you feel when you wake up? What's been bothering you?"

And just like that, we were on track.

Let me tell you something I've seen again and again: two people can lie down on the exact same mattress—one will sink into blissful comfort, and the other will look at me like, *"Are you kidding? This thing is awful."* And they're *both right.*

That's the secret most people miss when shopping for a mattress. There is no universally perfect mattress—there's only the perfect mattress *for you.* Your sleep needs are unique. Your body is unique. Your comfort preferences, sleep position, weight, temperature sensitivity, and health concerns all play a role. What feels like a cloud to one person might feel like a rock to someone else.

So if you've been frustrated by your mattress experience in the past—or if you've bought a "top-rated" bed that felt all wrong—you're not crazy. You were probably trying to fit your body into someone else's idea of comfort. In this chapter, we're going to break that pattern. We will help you understand what *you* need in a mattress to get the kind of sleep you've been chasing. Because once you know yourself, choosing the right mattress becomes a whole lot easier—and way more successful.

Know Thyself: Understanding Your Sleep Style

One of the first—and most important—steps in choosing the right mattress is understanding how you sleep. Most people don't think twice about their sleep position, but it actually has a massive impact on what kind of mattress will help you sleep better. Side sleeper? Back sleeper? Stomach sleeper? Combination of all three? Each position puts different pressure on your body, and your mattress has to respond to that.

Side sleepers, for example, tend to need more **pressure relief**—especially in the hips and shoulders. If the mattress is too firm, it can create painful pressure points that wake you up or keep you tossing and turning all night. On the other hand, **back sleepers** need more **support** to maintain natural spinal alignment, especially in the lower back. A mattress that's too soft can cause their hips to sink too deep, leading to lower back pain over time. **Stomach sleepers** (probably the most difficult position for healthy sleep) need a firm mattress to keep their spine from dipping too much, especially in the midsection. And then there are **combination sleepers**—people who change positions throughout the night. They usually need a mattress with good responsiveness that makes it easy to shift without disrupting sleep. They generally are side sleepers with pressure points - so something with high-density foams will be most helpful to reduce tossing and turning.

Most people never consider this, and they buy a mattress based on marketing or price instead of sleep style. But if your mattress doesn't match how you sleep, it's going to fight your body instead of supporting it. That's why knowing your sleep style isn't just helpful—it's essential. Your body has a natural rhythm, and when you honor it with the right mattress, sleep becomes easier, deeper, and far more refreshing.

Body Type and Weight – Why It Matters

Here's something else most people overlook when buying a mattress: **your body type and weight have a direct impact on how a mattress feels and performs**. It's not just about sleep position—it's also about how much pressure your body places on the mattress, how deeply you sink into the layers, and how the materials respond to your shape and weight. The same mattress will feel completely different to a 120-pound person than it will to someone who weighs 220 pounds. That's not a flaw in the mattress—it's just physics.

If you have a **lighter body frame**, you may find that many mattresses feel too firm. That's because your body isn't heavy enough to sink in and activate the comfort layers designed to relieve pressure. You'll need something with softer, more responsive materials that contour quickly and relieve tension without feeling like you're floating on top. On the other hand, if you have a **heavier**

frame, you need a mattress with more **durability and stronger support layers** to keep you properly aligned and prevent you from "bottoming out." Softer mattresses may feel good at first but can start to sag or lose their shape more quickly under extra weight, especially if the materials aren't high quality. However, it's not always necessarily true. Softer mattresses can outlast firmer mattresses if they are using High-Density foams. Softer mattresses can work for any weight of a person, especially side sleepers... but a pear-shaped person may need something firmer than a rectangle or hourglass-shaped person.

Then, there's body shape to consider. People with **broad shoulders, curvier hips,** or **narrow waists** often need specific zoning or extra pressure relief in key areas. That's why listening to how your body feels is so important—not just what the label says. Comfort isn't one-size-fits-all, and your mattress shouldn't be either. When you find one that's designed for your unique build, you'll not only sleep better—you'll *wake up* better, too.

Comfort Is Subjective (and That's Okay)

Let's settle something now: **comfort is personal**. What feels like the perfect mattress to your best friend might feel totally wrong to you—and that's not just okay; it's expected. There's no universal definition of comfort because everybody is different. Some people love that sink-in, hug-you feel of plush memory foam. Others feel trapped by it and prefer the bounce and support of a firmer hybrid mattress. Neither group is wrong. They just value different things—and that's the whole point.

The mattress world is full of marketing claims like "the most comfortable mattress in the world" or "universally perfect firmness." But here's the truth: there's *no such thing.* Comfort is influenced by your body weight, shape, sleep position, pain history, and experiences. (For example, if you grew up sleeping on a firm mattress, your body might associate firmness with comfort—even if something softer might serve you better now.) That's why listening to your body when testing mattresses is so important. Don't let a salesperson—or a 5-star review from a stranger—talk you out of what actually feels right for *you.*

So permit yourself to have an opinion. Trust your gut. Your comfort is not up for debate, and you're not being picky—you're being smart. You're making a decision that affects how you feel every morning and how you function every day. Your experience is the only one that matters when it comes to sleep.

Special Sleep Needs

While most mattress advice focuses on the average sleeper, the truth is **many people have unique needs that go far beyond the basics.** Maybe you're pregnant, living with chronic back pain, recovering from surgery, or dealing with arthritis. Maybe you're an athlete with muscle fatigue or a senior with joint sensitivity. Or maybe you're simply someone who sleeps hot, snores or shares a bed with someone who snores. All these factors can dramatically affect which mattress will actually help you sleep better.

For example, if you deal with **chronic pain or arthritis**, a mattress that offers both support and pressure relief is essential. Too firm, and you'll feel pain in your joints. Too soft, and your spine may fall out of alignment. If you're **pregnant**, you'll need a mattress that helps accommodate shifting weight and supports the hips and lower back without feeling too restrictive. If you're a **hot sleeper**, materials that trap heat—like dense foams without cooling technology—can make your nights miserable. You'll need breathable materials and cooling features to stay comfortable and asleep. And for **couples with different sleep needs**, split mattresses or mattresses with dual-sided firmness can be a game-changer.

The point is no two people sleep alike. Your lifestyle, health, and preferences all deserve to be part of the mattress decision. The more honest you are about your real-world sleep challenges, your mattress choice will be more successful. You're not just buying a bed—you're investing in a solution designed for *your* life.

The Myth of the "Magic Mattress"

It's easy to fall for the idea that there's a "magic mattress" out there—one perfect bed that will solve all your sleep problems, fix your back pain, and feel amazing from night one. You've seen the ads: glowing reviews, sleek videos, bold claims like *"the best sleep of your life"* or *"everyone's favorite mattress."* But here's the honest truth: **there is no perfect mattress for everyone.** That myth has caused a lot of frustration—and a lot of wasted money—for people chasing a promise that was never realistic in the first place.

Even the most expensive, high-tech mattress won't work if it's not the right fit for your body and your sleep style. A $10,000 bed might feel amazing to one person and completely wrong to someone else. That doesn't mean the mattress is bad—it just means it's not *your* match. The real key to finding the right mattress isn't about chasing hype—it's about understanding your body, your needs, and how you actually sleep.

So instead of searching for the so-called "best mattress," start looking for the *best mattress for you*. One that supports your spine relieves your pressure points, regulates your temperature, and fits your lifestyle. That's where the real magic happens—not in a brand name or a flashy commercial, but in a bed that finally lets you rest the way you were meant to.

The Goal: Find *Your* Match

At the end of the day, choosing a mattress isn't about impressing anyone or chasing trends—it's about finding *your* match. It's about tuning into your body, listening to what it needs, and refusing to settle for something that doesn't support your rest, health, and peace of mind. This is where your sleep journey becomes personal. You're not just shopping—you're building the foundation for better nights, better mornings, and a better life.

When you find the right mattress, everything changes. You fall asleep faster. You stay asleep longer. Your body relaxes, your mind quiets, and your mornings start with clarity instead of grogginess. That's the power of a mattress that's built for *you*. Now that you understand your body, your sleep style, and the key elements that make or break your rest, you're ready to take the next step.

In the next chapter, we're going to get practical. I'll walk you through exactly **how to shop for a mattress**— what to look for, what to avoid, how to test a bed properly, and how to make sure you're investing in something that will truly change how you sleep. This is where knowledge turns into action. Let's find your perfect fit.

5

Mattress Shopping 101

YOU'RE BROWSING THE showroom floor, surrounded by dozens of seemingly identical white rectan-
gles. A salesperson approaches with a cheerful smile and
asks what you're looking for. And suddenly, you freeze.
What *are* you looking for? They all look the same. They
all promise the same thing. And the prices are all over the
map. How are you supposed to know which one is right?

If this sounds familiar, you're not alone. I've spent over
two decades watching people walk into mattress stores
with a mixture of hope and dread on their faces. They know
sleep matters—they know they need a better mattress—
but they have no idea how to navigate the sea of options
in front of them. They feel overwhelmed, confused, and
worried about making an expensive mistake.

I get it. Mattress shopping can feel like trying to
buy a car without knowing how to drive. The industry
doesn't always make it easy, with confusing terminology,
conflicting advice, and sales tactics that can leave your
head spinning. But it doesn't have to be that way. In fact,
once you know what to look for and what to ignore,

buying a mattress becomes a whole lot simpler—and a whole lot more successful.

In this chapter, I'm going to pull back the curtain. I'll show you exactly what matters when choosing a mattress, the questions you should ask (and the ones you can skip), and how to cut through the marketing noise to find what your body actually needs. Think of this as your insider's guide—the real talk that most salespeople won't give you but that will save you time, money, and a whole lot of headaches. Let's dive in and make this process painless.

What to Look For First: Breaking Down Mattress Materials

Before you even step foot in a store or start browsing online, you need to understand what mattresses are actually made of. Each material has its own unique feel, benefits, and limitations—and knowing the basics will help you navigate your options with confidence.

Memory Foam Mattresses

Memory foam has become wildly popular over the last decade, and for good reason. It's known for that "hug" feeling—the way it slowly contours to your body's shape and relieves pressure points. Memory foam was originally developed by NASA to cushion astronauts during takeoff, and that pressure-relieving quality is what makes it so effective for sleep.

Memory foam mattresses work well for side sleepers who need that extra give around shoulders and hips. They're also great for couples because they absorb movement—meaning your partner's midnight bathroom trip won't wake you up. The downside? Traditional memory foam can trap heat, and some people feel "stuck" in the mattress or find it difficult to change positions. Newer memory foams have addressed many of these issues with cooling technologies and more responsive formulations.

It's also worth noting - memory foam tends to feel a touch firmer, and you can err on the side of firmer and still get some pressure relief.

Innerspring Mattresses

This is the classic mattress most of us grew up with—metal coils providing bounce and support. Innerspring mattresses have evolved significantly over the years. Modern versions often feature individually wrapped coils (sometimes called pocket coils) that move independently, reducing motion transfer while still providing that traditional responsive feel.

Innerspring mattresses tend to sleep cooler since air can flow freely between the coils. They also provide excellent edge support—meaning you can sit or sleep near the edge without feeling like you're going to roll off. The downside? They may not offer enough pressure relief for side sleepers or people with joint pain, and lower-quality versions can develop squeaks or sags over time. The downside is that many of these don't come with a lot of specialty foams and fibers, which translates to a less comfortable life. This means it starts underperforming (loses its ability to relieve pressure) faster than other beds that have memory foam, latex, or natural fibers in the bed.

Latex Mattresses

Latex is a natural material derived from rubber tree sap (though synthetic versions also exist). It has a unique, responsive feel—offering pressure relief without the sinking feeling of memory foam. It bounces back quickly when you move, making it easier to shift positions throughout the night.

Latex mattresses are incredibly durable, often lasting 15+ years with proper care. They are durable due to their rubber-based nature, and they are more breathable than polyurethane foams. They're naturally resistant to dust mites and mold, making them a good choice for allergy sufferers. Many latex mattresses are also made with organic materials, appealing to environmentally conscious shoppers.

Hybrid Mattresses

As the name suggests, hybrid mattresses combine different materials—typically coils for support with foam or latex comfort layers on top. This "best of both worlds" approach aims to maximize benefits while minimizing drawbacks. However, the term "Hybrid" is the most convoluted term in the industry. It's so overused because it is a "hot button" word for many shoppers. So, shoppers need to be careful when they are told something is a hybrid. It should combine two major Technologies, coils for support, and at least 50% or more should be SPECIALTY foam (memory foam or latex or a combo).

A well-designed hybrid can offer the pressure relief of specialty foam beds with the breathability and responsiveness of coils. They tend to work well for a wide range of sleep styles, making them versatile options for couples with different preferences. It's important to check what's actually inside—some lower-quality "hybrids" are mostly springs with only a thin comfort layer on top.

Adjustable Air Beds

These high-tech options let you control firmness by adding or removing air from the chambers inside the mattress. Many models allow each side of the bed to be adjusted separately, making them ideal for couples with different comfort preferences.

The ability to change firmness levels can be helpful for people with fluctuating needs—like pregnancy or recovery from injury. The downside? Many of them are dependent on the person knowing exactly what they want and need to make the right changes, which can be challenging to some.

A Note About Materials and Quality

Here's something most people don't realize: the quality of materials matters far more than the type of materials. A high-quality innerspring will outperform a low-quality memory foam any day. When you're evaluating a mattress, ask about the density of the foams, the gauge of the coils, and the overall construction. Higher-density foams (3.5+ pounds per cubic foot for memory foam, 1.5+ for conventional polyfoam) will last longer and provide better support. Look for mattresses with multiple layers designed for specific functions—support, transition, comfort, and cooling.

And remember—don't get too caught up in buzz-words or proprietary technologies. Every brand has its own fancy-sounding foams and features, but what really matters is how the mattress feels to you and how well it's constructed to last.

Key Questions to Ask: What to Ask Salespeople, What to Read in Reviews

Once you understand the basic materials, it's time to dig deeper. Whether you're talking to a salesperson or reading online reviews, asking the right questions can help you cut through the marketing hype and find the information that actually matters for your sleep.

Questions for Salespeople

The #1 most important question is: What will this mattress DO for me? You want to know if it will relieve more pressure and be more supportive than your previous mattress. Other good questions to ask include:

1. **"What's inside this mattress?"** This basic question reveals a lot. A knowledgeable salesperson

should be able to explain the specific materials, layers, and construction details—not just vague marketing terms. If they can't tell you the density of the foams or the gauge of the coils, that's a red flag.

2. **"How does this mattress handle heat?"** Temperature regulation is crucial for good sleep. Ask about specific cooling technologies—not just buzzwords like "cool sleeping," but actual features like gel infusion, phase change materials, or breathable covers.

3. **"What kind of foundation does this mattress need?"** Some mattresses require specific foundations or will void their warranty if used on the wrong base. Ask whether a box spring, platform bed, or adjustable base is recommended.

4. **"What is your return policy, and how does it work?"** This is absolutely critical. Find out how long the trial period is, whether there are any fees for returns, and exactly how the return process works. Some companies make returns easy; others make it a nightmare.

5. **"What is covered under the warranty?"** A long warranty period means nothing if it doesn't cover the issues you're likely to encounter. Ask specifically what's covered, what would void the warranty, and how claims are processed.

6. **"How long will this mattress maintain its comfort and support?"** This question often reveals more honest information than asking

about the lifespan. Many salespeople will tell you a mattress will "last" 10 years, but the comfort might deteriorate much sooner.

What to Look for in Reviews

Online reviews can be helpful, but they can also be very misleading if you don't know what to look for. Here's how to get the most value from reviews:

1. **Look for reviewers with similar needs.** A review from someone with your height, weight, sleep position, and concerns will be far more relevant than generic ratings.
2. **Pay attention to long-term reviews.** Many people review mattresses after just a few nights—but the real test is how they feel after months of use. Look for updates to original reviews or specifically seek out longer-term feedback.
3. **Watch for specific complaints.** Vague praise like "best sleep ever" is less helpful than specific feedback like "relieved my shoulder pain" or "started to sag after 18 months."
4. **Be skeptical of extreme reviews.** Both overly glowing 5-star reviews and scathing 1-star complaints often represent outliers rather than typical experiences.
5. **Look for patterns across multiple reviews.** If you see the same praise or complaint mentioned by multiple reviewers, it's more likely to be a true characteristic of the mattress.

But remember, no mattress works for everyone, so even the highest-rated bed will have some negative reviews. What matters is whether the common praise and complaints align with your specific needs and concerns. So be very cautious when reading reviews!

In-Store vs. Online: Pros and Cons of Each

The mattress shopping landscape has changed dramatically in recent years. Once, buying a mattress meant spending hours in a showroom. Today, direct-to-consumer online mattress companies have transformed the industry. Both approaches have their strengths and weaknesses—and knowing them can help you decide which is right for you.

In-store shopping offers an undeniable sensory advantage. You can stretch out on each mattress, compare models side by side, and decide in seconds whether that pillow top feels plush or just puffy. A seasoned sales-person—if you find a good one—can watch how you settle in, ask about your sleep position, and steer you toward constructions that match your pressure relief or support needs. Finally, if your current bed has collapsed and you need relief tonight, many stores can dispatch a mattress the same day or at least by tomorrow, sparing you to wait for a boxed bed to arrive and expand.

Still, showrooms come with downsides. Sales pressure can be intense, and five minutes of awkward reclining under fluorescent lights is a poor proxy for eight hours of real sleep. Manufacturers muddy the waters further by rebranding essentially identical models for different chains, so comparison shopping turns into an exercise in decoding aliases.

Buying online flips many of those variables. You can browse specs, pore over customer reviews, and check competing prices without anyone angling for a commission. Nearly every direct-to-consumer brand backs the purchase with a triple-digit trial period, giving you three months or more to decide if the mattress works in your own bedroom, not just on a showroom floor.

The drawback, of course, is the leap of faith: you commit before you've ever felt the surface. If the match proves wrong, returns are usually free but still a hassle; some companies ask you to arrange a donation and submit paperwork before they issue a refund. Customer support happens through chat or phone, which can't replicate an expert physically tailoring options to your feedback. And if you need a mattress tonight, waiting several days for shipping—and a few more for full expansion—may not be feasible. In short, online buying maximizes convenience and price clarity, while in-store shopping maximizes tactile certainty and instant gratification; the best option depends on which trade-offs matter most to you.

Which Approach Is Right for You?

There's no one-size-fits-all answer here. If you're confident in your preferences and comfortable making big purchases online, the direct-to-consumer route might be perfect. If you're new to mattress shopping or have specific needs that require expert guidance, an in-store experience might be worth the potential premium.

Many people now take a hybrid approach. They research online, test mattresses in stores to narrow down preferences, and then make their final purchase wherever it offers the best value. The key is to use each channel's strengths while minimizing its weaknesses.

Common Pitfalls: Budget Mistakes, Falling for Hype, Ignoring Personal Needs

After helping thousands of people find the right mattress, I've seen the same mistakes pop up again and again. These pitfalls can turn what should be an exciting purchase into a frustrating experience—and leave you sleeping on a mattress that's all wrong for your body. Let's address them head-on so you can avoid these common traps.

Budget Mistake #1: Focusing Only on Initial Price

One of the biggest mistakes I see is people shopping solely by price point. Yes, budget matters—but when you calculate the cost per night over the lifespan of a mattress, the difference between a $3,000 mattress and a $10,000 mattress might be just pennies per night. And if that higher-quality mattress lasts twice as long, it's actually the better value in the long run.

A better approach is to look at the price per year of expected quality use. If a $1,200 mattress stays comfortable for 8 years, that's $150 per year. If a $600 mattress only stays comfortable for 3 years, that's $200 per year—making the more expensive mattress the better long-term value.

The Hype Trap: Falling for Marketing Claims

The mattress industry is notorious for buzzwords and proprietary technologies that sound revolutionary but often amount to minor variations on standard materials. "Cooling crystals," "sleep science," "pressure-eliminating technology"—these terms might sound impressive but tell you very little about how the mattress will actually feel or perform.

Instead of focusing on marketing language, look at the actual specifications: the density of foams, the type and arrangement of coils, the overall construction, and materials. These tangible details will tell you far more about quality and durability than fancy terminology.

Ignoring Your Body's Feedback

Sometimes, we talk ourselves into a mattress that doesn't actually feel right. Maybe it's a great idea, or a friend loves it, or it has amazing reviews—so we ignore the signals our body is sending. If something doesn't feel comfortable in the store, it probably won't magically become comfortable at home. Trust your body over reviews, recommendations, or even the most convincing salesperson.

Remember Karen from earlier in this book? The woman who came in convinced she needed a firm mattress because "everyone says it's best for your back"? She eventually purchased a medium-firm mattress with extra pressure relief in the shoulder area—and later told me it was the best sleep she'd had in years. Your body knows what it needs. Listen to it.

The Comparison Confusion

Another common pitfall is trying to compare identical models across different retailers. As I mentioned earlier, manufacturers often create "exclusive" models for different stores—changing the name, adding a different cover fabric, or making minor adjustments to the internal layers. This practice makes true comparison shopping nearly impossible.

Instead of trying to find the exact same mattress at different retailers, focus on finding the right type of mattress for your needs and then compare similar options based on specifications and value. Don't get caught up in thinking there's one perfect mattress that you need to find at the best possible price.

Making Sleep an Afterthought

Perhaps the biggest mistake people make is not prioritizing sleep in the first place. They'll spend thousands on a TV, a couch, or kitchen upgrades—things they use for hours a day—but balk at investing in a quality mattress they'll spend a third of their life on.

Think about it: you spend more time on your mattress than any other furniture in your home. It directly impacts your health, your mood, your productivity, and your quality of life. If there's one home purchase worth thoughtful consideration and appropriate investment, it's your mattress.

The Art of the Trial: How to Test a Mattress Properly

Whether you're stretching out on mattresses in a showroom or settling one into place for an at-home trial, the way you test determines whether you'll live with a dream bed or an expensive regret. In a store, dress for the job: loose, comfortable clothing lets you sink in naturally, whereas tight jeans or a stiff jacket can skew your perception of firmness. Give your top contenders a genuine audition—about ten minutes, not a cursory thirty-second flop. Climb into your usual sleep position, rotate to a few others, and notice how the surface cradles your shoulders and hand ips and holds up the lower back. If you share a bed, bring your partner so you can judge motion transfer and overall space together; feel free to ask the salesperson to strip away those showroom comforters and decorative shams so you're evaluating the mattress with just a sheet and a pillow similar to what you use at home.

An at-home trial calls for equal diligence, just in slower motion. Slip a waterproof, breathable protector over the mattress the first night—most return policies require the bed to be spotless—and then commit to at least two or three weeks before you render a verdict. Bodies often need time to adjust, and what feels odd on night one may feel sublime by night twenty. Keep informal notes on how you feel each morning: Are aches easing? Do you fall asleep within 15 minutes? Does your partner's tossing still wake you? Observe the bed under different conditions—hot and cool nights, sore-muscle days, and evenings when you're bone-tired or wide-awake—to see how it behaves across real-life variables. Finally, be ruthlessly honest. If you're consistently waking up stiffer or more fatigued despite your best efforts, trust the data, not the marketing. A mattress that doesn't serve your body—no matter how glowing the reviews—should go back in the box.

Remember, a good mattress feels different to different people. What matters most is not what others think of it but how it affects your sleep quality night after night. Trust your experience over any review, recommendation, or sales pitch.

Making the Final Decision: Balancing Quality, Price, and Personal Comfort

After all the research, testing, and consideration, how do you finally pull the trigger on such an important purchase? Here's my framework for making the final decision with confidence—balancing all the factors that matter without getting overwhelmed.

Step 1: Prioritize Your Non-Negotiables

Start by identifying the 2-3 factors that are absolute must-haves for you. These might include:

- Pressure relief for chronic shoulder pain
- Minimal motion transfer if your partner tosses and turns
- Temperature regulation: if you sleep hot
- Sustainable or organic materials if you have chemical sensitivities or room environmental concerns
- Edge support if you use the full surface of the mattress

Whatever your top priorities are, make these the foundation of your decision. Any mattress that doesn't meet these core needs should be eliminated, regardless of price or other features.

Step 2: Set a Realistic Budget Range

Instead of a fixed price point, establish a range that represents what you're willing to spend for a good night's sleep. Remember to think in terms of value over time rather than upfront cost. A quality mattress that helps you sleep better for years is worth stretching your budget a bit if necessary.

If your budget is truly limited, consider timing your purchase around major sale periods (Memorial Day, Labor Day, Black Friday) when mattress discounts are deepest. Also, look into financing options—many retailers offer 0% interest if paid within a certain period, which can make a quality mattress more accessible.

Step 3: Narrow to 2-3 Final Contenders

Based on your priorities and budget, narrow your options to just 2-3 final contenders. This prevents decision fatigue and allows you to compare specific features rather than feeling overwhelmed by endless options.

For each contender, make a simple pros and cons list. Be specific about what you liked and any concerns you have. Sometimes, seeing these factors written down makes the right choice much clearer.

Step 4: Consider the Complete Package

A smart mattress purchase considers more than the surface you sleep on. The surrounding policies and services can make or break long-term satisfaction. Start with the warranty: its length matters, but so do the details—what defects qualify and how quickly replacements arrive. Next, weigh the trial period and return process. Ninety or 120 nights mean little if sending the mattress back requires elaborate packaging or donation paperwork, whereas a streamlined, no-questions exchange builds genuine safety into the purchase. Delivery and setup also influence real-world value. White-glove service that installs the new bed and hauls away the old one can save you an afternoon of heavy lifting and disposal fees. Finally, scan customer service reviews to see how the company handles hiccups months or years down the line. When two mattresses feel equally good, the one backed by a responsive support team and friction-free policies often proves the better investment—even if its upfront price is a tad higher.

Step 5: Trust Your Body, Not Just Reviews

At the end of the day, your personal comfort trumps everything else. If a mattress feels right to you but has mixed reviews, go with your experience. If a highly-rated mattress doesn't feel comfortable, trust your body over the ratings.

Remember, you're the one who will be sleeping on this mattress every night. Your comfort, your sleep quality, and your satisfaction are what matter most. Reviews can provide useful information, but they can't tell you how your unique body will respond to a particular mattress.

Step 6: Make Peace with Imperfection

Here's a truth that might actually help you make a decision: there is no perfect mattress. Every option involves some compromise, whether in features, price, or convenience. The goal isn't to find perfection—it's to find the best match for your specific needs and preferences.

Once you've done your research, tested thoroughly, and considered all the relevant factors, make your choice with confidence. And remember, most quality mattresses come with generous trial periods, giving you the ultimate safety net to ensure you've made the right decision.

Your Mattress Shopping Checklist

When you head out to choose a new mattress, start by taking stock of your personal sleep profile: note whether you're a side, back, stomach, or combination sleeper; estimate your weight and temperature preferences; and list any special needs such as chronic pain, allergies, or CPAP use. Clarify what you want the bed to do for you—perhaps pressure relief for achy joints, zoned support for spinal alignment, strong motion isolation for a restless partner, or dependable edge support for easy exits. With priorities in hand, settle on a realistic budget that reflects long-term value rather than just the sticker price.

Next, dig into each mattress's guts. Learn which foams, coils, or latex layers it uses and how those materials influence durability, cooling, and overall feel. When you test contenders—whether in a store or during an at-home trial—give each one ample time in your real sleep positions and zero in on any budding pressure points. As you evaluate models, pepper the salesperson or online rep with practical questions: What exactly does the warranty cover, how painless is the return process, and does the company offer white-glove delivery or removal of your old bed?

Finally, weigh the whole package. A mattress backed by responsive customer service, straightforward policies, and hassle-free delivery often outperforms a cheaper option that skimps on support after the sale. Above all, trust the signals your body sends; personal comfort is the ultimate pass-fail test no spreadsheet or review can replace.

With this approach, you'll be well-equipped to navigate the mattress shopping process with confidence—whether you're browsing online or visiting a showroom. Remember, this isn't just a purchase; it's an investment in your health, well-being, and quality of life. It deserves careful consideration and appropriate priority.

In our next chapter, we'll move beyond the mattress itself to explore your entire sleep environment. Because while the right mattress is the foundation of great sleep, your bedroom as a whole plays a crucial role in how well you rest each night. We'll discuss everything from pillows and sheets to lighting, temperature, and design—creating a true sleep sanctuary that supports deep, restorative sleep every night.

6

Creating Your Sleep Sanctuary

A WHILE BACK, my wife and I sat down and had one of those practical but surprisingly important conversations—how to turn our bedroom into a real *sleep sanctuary*. Not just a place where we sleep but a space that actually *helps* us sleep. We realized that as much as we knew about mattresses, our environment was still working against us.

So we made some changes.

First, we swapped out our old curtains for blackout ones. It was amazing how much better we slept just by blocking out the early morning light, and that glow from the streetlamp outside. Next, we replaced our bright digital clock with one that didn't light up the room like a landing strip. We also made a firm decision: no more phones in the bedroom. They now charge overnight in the hallway—no late-night scrolling, no buzzing notifications, no temptation.

We also unplugged the TV. It's still there, but it only gets used when one of us is sick in bed. Otherwise, our room is for rest—not for Netflix binges. And instead of waking up to a blaring alarm, we switched to one of those sunrise clocks that slowly lit up the room. It's a small change, but it makes a huge difference—our mornings feel calmer less jolting.

All these shifts helped create an atmosphere of peace. But here's what I've learned: **you can make your room pitch-black, silent, cool, and clutter-free—but if your mattress isn't right for your body, the rest won't help much.** Comfort, support, and pressure relief are the foundation. Everything else just enhances the experience. Your sleep environment matters, but your mattress still does the heavy lifting.

This conversation captures something I've noticed over and over again: we often create bedrooms that look great in photos but don't actually support great sleep. We focus on aesthetics while overlooking the elements that truly influence rest. The truth is, your bedroom should be more than just a beautiful space—it should be a sleep sanctuary deliberately designed to help your body and mind transition from the chaos of the day into deep, restorative sleep.

In the previous chapter, we talked about choosing the right mattress—the foundation of good sleep. But even the perfect mattress can't overcome an environment that works against your rest. Your bedroom as a whole plays a critical role in how quickly you fall asleep, how deeply you sleep, and how refreshed you feel in the morning. Everything from temperature and lighting to your pillows and even the clutter on your nightstand can either promote or prevent quality sleep.

The good news? Creating a sleep sanctuary doesn't require an interior design degree or a massive budget. It's about making intentional choices that signal to your brain and body that it's time to rest. In this chapter, we'll explore how to transform your bedroom from just another room in your house into a true haven for sleep—a place that helps you disconnect from the stress of the day and reconnect with the peace your body and mind need.

Room Environment: Temperature, Lighting, Sound, and Décor

Your sleep environment affects your rest far more than most people realize. In fact, your brain is constantly processing environmental cues—even while you sleep—and these signals either help your body relax or keep it on alert. Let's look at the four key elements of your sleep environment and how to optimize each for better rest.

Temperature: The Goldilocks Zone

Did you know that your bedroom temperature might be just as important as your mattress when it comes to quality sleep? It's true. Your body temperature naturally drops as part of the sleep process, and a room that's too warm can interfere with this essential cooling.

The ideal sleep temperature for most people is between 65-68°F (18-20°C)—cooler than many people keep in their homes. If that sounds chilly, remember that you'll be under covers, and your body generates heat while you sleep. A slightly cool room helps your core temperature decrease, which triggers deeper sleep.

Here's how to create the optimal temperature environment:

- **Program your thermostat** to drop a few degrees at bedtime if possible
- **Layer your bedding** so you can adjust throughout the night if needed
- **Consider cooling technologies** like breathable mattress covers or pillows with cooling properties if you tend to sleep hot.
- **Use a fan** for both air circulation and gentle white noise
- **Keep hot electronics** out of the bedroom, as they generate heat

Temperature issues are often the hidden culprit behind restless nights. If you're kicking off covers, waking up sweaty, or feeling stifled, adjusting your room temperature could be the simple fix you've been missing.

Lighting: Respect Your Rhythm

Light isn't just about being able to see—it's one of the primary ways your body knows when to be awake and when to sleep. Your brain has an internal clock (connected to your circadian rhythm) that relies heavily on light cues. When your eyes detect darkness, your brain triggers the release of melatonin, the hormone that helps you fall asleep. When they detect light—especially the blue light from phones, tablets, and other screens—melatonin production is suppressed, keeping you alert even when you're tired.

Light is one of the strongest cues the brain uses to judge when it should be alert and when it can safely slip into sleep, so shaping your evening environment pays immediate dividends. About an hour before bed, begin dimming household lights to mimic the gradual loss of daylight; this drop in brightness nudges your internal clock to start releasing melatonin. Swap overhead fixtures for low-wattage lamps and choose warm-hued bulbs rather than cool "daylight" varieties, which can trick the brain into thinking it is still mid-afternoon. As you approach bedtime, eliminate stray glimmers that can undo the effect. Block street lamps and early-morning sun with true blackout curtains, or slip on a well-fitting sleep mask—an especially valuable tool for anyone living in brightly lit cities or rotating through night shifts. Scan the room for tiny LEDs on chargers, routers, or power strips and cover them with tape or opaque stickers so they don't pierce the darkness. Finally, keep phones, tablets, and laptops out of the bedroom if you can; if not, engage night-mode filters and power them down at least an hour before lights out. These simple adjustments create the deep, cave-like darkness your biology expects, making it far easier to fall asleep and stay there until morning.

Many people underestimate how sensitive our bodies are to light. Even the glow from a digital alarm clock can be enough to disrupt sleep for some people. Creating true darkness in your bedroom can lead to dramatically deeper and more refreshing sleep.

Sound: The Quiet (or Consistent) Comfort
Our brains continue to process sounds even during sleep, which is why a sudden noise can jolt you awake. The ideal sound environment isn't necessarily complete silence (though that works well for some people). What matters most is consistency—no sudden, unpredictable noises that trigger your brain's alert response.

For many people, especially light sleepers or those in noisy environments, a consistent background sound actually improves sleep by masking disruptive noises. Try using a white noise machine or fans to create consistent background sound. Or try nature sounds like rainfall or ocean waves if white noise feels too harsh. Consider earplugs if your environment is unpredictably noisy or if you have a snoring partner. Address squeaky floors or doors that might wake you when someone moves around. Position your bed away from shared walls if you live in an apartment or shared space.

Remember, the goal isn't absolute silence (unless that's what works for you)—it's creating a sound environment that helps your brain stay in deeper stages of sleep without constantly being pulled into alertness by unexpected noises.

Décor: Calm, Not Chaotic
Your bedroom's visual environment affects your ability to relax and transition into sleep. While this is the

most personal aspect of your sleep sanctuary, there are some general principles that help create a more restful space. Choose calming colors like soft blues, greens, or neutral tones rather than energizing ones like bright red or orange. Minimize visual clutter by keeping surfaces clear and having adequate storage. Select artwork that promotes calm rather than pieces that provoke strong emotional responses. Position your bed so you feel secure (many people sleep better when their bed is against a wall rather than floating in the middle of a room). Keep work-related items out of sight to create a mental separation between sleep and stress.

Your bedroom should feel like a retreat from the world—a place where your mind can let go of the day's pressures and truly relax. This doesn't mean it can't reflect your personality or style, but the overall effect should be calming rather than stimulating.

For Lisa, my friend with the beautiful but not restful bedroom, we made several simple changes: installing room-darkening curtains behind her decorative ones, removing the bright alarm clock, adding a small fan for both cooling and gentle background noise, and clearing the work files from her bedside table. Within a week, she reported falling asleep faster and waking up less during the night—all without sacrificing the beautiful aesthetics she'd worked so hard to create.

Bedding Basics: Choosing the Right Pillows, Sheets, and Blankets

While your mattress forms the foundation of your sleep setup, your bedding plays a crucial supporting role. The right pillows, sheets, and blankets can enhance comfort, regulate temperature, and help your body maintain proper alignment throughout the night. Let's break down how to choose each element for optimal sleep.

Pillows: Support Where You Need It

The ideal pillow has less to do with price or lofty fluff and everything to do with how well it supports your head and neck in your usual sleep position. If the pillow is too tall, your neck tilts upward; if it is too flat, your head falls back—either scenario can trigger strain, headaches, and fitful sleep. Side sleepers need the most loft and firmness because the pillow must bridge the distance between shoulder and ear to keep the spine level; models labeled for side sleeping or designed with high gussets usually fit the bill. Back sleepers fare best with a medium-height pillow that cushions the natural curve of the neck without pitching the head forward—contoured memory foam or latex designs are reliable choices. Stomach sleepers, by contrast, require the thinnest, softest option—sometimes no head pillow at all—to prevent neck hyper-extension; many find greater relief by sliding a slim pillow under the hips instead, which eases pressure on the lower back. Combination sleepers, who shift positions through the night, benefit from pillows that reshape easily, such as shredded foam fills or adjustable models that let you add or remove stuffing to taste.

Beyond your primary pillow, targeted supports can solve special problems. A small knee pillow between the legs helps side sleepers reduce hip torque and lower-back tension. Wedge pillows elevate the torso to curb acid reflux or open the airway for easier breathing, while full-length body pillows offer head-to-ankle alignment—a blessing during pregnancy or for anyone nursing sore joints. Keep in mind that even a premium pillow has a finite life: materials compress, foams break down, and allergens accumulate. Expect to replace most pillows every one to two years, and sooner if you wake with new neck pain or find yourself constantly fluffing and folding in search of lost support.

Sheets: The Comfort Layer

Because sheets are the only part of the bed that stays in direct contact with your skin for eight hours straight, their fabric and construction make a bigger difference to sleep quality than most people realize. Thread-count marketing can be seductive, but fiber quality matters far more: a 400-thread-count sheet woven from long-staple Pima, Supima, or Egyptian cotton will breathe and soften beautifully, whereas an 800-count sheet spun from short, coarse fibers can feel hot and scratchy. Natural bamboo viscose rivals cotton for smoothness yet outperforms it at wicking moisture, making it a favorite of hot sleepers. Linen, prized for centuries, offers unparalleled airflow and rugged durability; its slightly nubbly texture softens with every wash and excels on sultry summer nights. Even budget-friendly microfiber has its place, though you trade some breathability for the lower price.

Weave dictates hand-feel and thermal behavior. A percale weave—think of the crisp snap of a freshly pressed dress shirt—stays cool and matte, ideal for warm climates or sweaty sleepers. Sateen drapes more heavily, feels silkier, and traps a bit more warmth thanks to its lustrous, four-over-one yarn pattern. Jersey knit sheets stretch like a favorite T-shirt, cocooning you in softness, while brushed flannel builds a fluffy nap that holds heat on frosty nights.

Match those characteristics to your own temperature tendencies. If you routinely kick off the covers, reach for lightweight percale cotton or bamboo in the warmer months, then swap to the same fabrics in linen or sateen as the seasons cool. If you shiver easily, flannel or heavy-weight sateen can create a cozy microclimate without piling on extra blankets. Many households keep separate summer and winter sheet sets for exactly this reason: rotating fabrics to align with the thermometer stabilizes sleep and reduces nocturnal tossing.

In short, if you find yourself waking sweaty, itchy, or inexplicably restless, the culprit may be less your mattress than the sheet set wrapped around it. Investing in breathable, skin-friendly fibers and seasonally appropriate weaves is a small change that can pay immediate dividends in deeper, more comfortable sleep.

Blankets and Comforters: Layered for Comfort

Your blanket system should act like a climate-control dial you can adjust without fully waking. Because body temperature drifts downward in the early nighttime hours and rises again toward morning, layering is the simplest way to stay comfortable: start with a breathable top sheet, add lightweight cotton or micro-quilt for mild insulation, and keep a loftier comforter or duvet within reach for the chilliest stretches. Natural fills outperform synthetics at regulating warmth. Down (or a high-quality down alternative) delivers remarkable heat-to-weight efficiency. Cotton breathes effortlessly and launders easily, while wool—often underestimated—insulates on winter nights yet wicks moisture to feel surprisingly cool in summer.

Weight and pressure deserve equal consideration. Some sleepers relax under the gentle, even heft of a weighted blanket—usually about ten percent of one's body weight—because the steady pressure calms the nervous system and reduces midnight fidgeting. Others find any heavy covering claustrophobic and rest better with airy layers they can flip off in seconds. Blanket dimensions matter, too: if two people share the bed, over-sized covers prevent the nightly tug-of-war that shreds sleep for both partners.

Finally, recognize that thermal comfort is personal. When one sleeper runs hotter than the other, a "split" strategy—separate blankets or duvets for each side—eliminates compromise and keeps peace in the bed. By tailoring layers, materials, and weight to individual needs, you create a flexible micro-environment that lets everyone drift through the night undisturbed.

Mattress Protection: The Hidden Essential

A high-quality mattress protector may not feel as glamorous as new sheets or a plush duvet, but it is the unsung hero of a healthy bed. By forming a waterproof yet breathable barrier over the sleep surface, it shields the mattress from spills, sweat, and everyday grime that can shorten its lifespan or void the warranty—most manufacturers refuse claims once a stain appears. That same barrier helps keep dust-mite debris, pet dander, and pollen from settling into the foam, easing nighttime allergies. Some models include full encasement that discourages bed-bug infestations. Modern protectors rely on technical membranes that repel liquids while still allowing air to circulate, so they regulate temperature instead of trapping body heat or crackling like old-fashioned plastic pads. Investing in one of these quiet, cool covers preserves your mattress investment, safeguards your health, and does it all without altering the comfort you chose in the first place.

Decluttering and Design: Simple Strategies to Make Your Bedroom a Haven

A cluttered bedroom creates a cluttered mind—and that's the last thing you need when trying to wind down for sleep. Beyond the obvious aesthetic impact, clutter affects sleep in surprising ways: it can increase stress hormones, create subconscious feelings of work left undone, and literally gather dust that impacts breathing and allergies. Let's look at how to create a space that promotes rather than prevents good sleep.

The Psychology of Bedroom Clutter

Your brain is constantly scanning your environment, even when you're not consciously aware of it. When your bedroom is filled with distractions—piles of laundry, work papers, exercise equipment—your brain registers these as potential tasks or concerns. This can make it difficult to mentally disconnect and transition into sleep mode.

Additionally, waking up to visual chaos starts your day with a subtle but real sense of being overwhelmed. By contrast, a tidy, intentional space helps your mind relax and signals that this room is for rest, not productivity or storage.

Begin by wiping the slate clean. If your bedroom has morphed into a catch-all for everything from unopened mail to half-finished craft projects, imagine—or literally enact—removing everything except the bed and a few indispensable pieces of furniture. Then, item by item, ask a single clarifying question before anything returns: "Does this object contribute to rest and sleep?" If the answer is no, give it a new home elsewhere. Be candid about hobby gear, workout equipment, or home-office overflow that has drifted inside; shifting them out instantly reclaims visual and mental breathing room. Essentials such as clothing, shoes, and personal items deserve designated storage so they won't migrate to floors and night table tops. The goal isn't austerity for its own sake; it's intentionality—inviting only those possessions that reinforce, rather than sabotage, your capacity to unwind.

Design choices should follow function. Position the bed where hallway light or door swings won't jolt you awake and where you won't bang a shin on a dresser during a groggy trip to the bathroom. Arrange furniture so clear pathways remain, and route charging cords so they don't turn into nocturnal snare traps. Thoughtfully organized closets prevent spillover that clutters the main room, while a streamlined bedside setup—lamp, book, water, perhaps a journal—keeps necessities within reach without turning the nightstand into a miniature junk drawer. Beauty still matters, but it should serve ease of movement and simplicity of routine, not impede them.

Once the room is reset, a handful of micro-habits will preserve the sense of calm. Making the bed each morning signals intention and discourages later clutter. Adopt a "one-in, one-out" rule so new purchases or gifts don't accumulate unchecked. Spend two or three minutes before lights out, putting stray items back where they belong. Keep a small tray or basket for things that need redistribution elsewhere in the house. Rotate seasonal clothing promptly instead of letting off-season garments pile up. These small gestures aren't perfectionism; they're investments in a space that consistently welcomes rest.

Finally, tackle the most pervasive form of clutter: digital devices. Phones, tablets, laptops, and TVs may be slim, but they monopolize mental real estate, flooding the room with blue light that suppresses melatonin, delivering stimulating content, and linking the bed to work or social media rather than sleep. Consider declaring the bedroom a low-tech zone—charge phones in another room or at least across the room, remove or disguise the television, and set strict boundaries for work devices. A "parking spot" near the bedroom door lets you keep gadgets accessible without letting them into the sleep sanctuary itself. This single adjustment—curbing technology's reach— often yields the most dramatic improvement, recasting your bedroom as a refuge devoted to restoration rather than an extension of daytime demands.

Investing in the Long Haul: When to Splurge vs. Where to Save

Creating a sleep sanctuary doesn't have to break the bank, but certain elements are worth investing in, while others offer opportunities to save. Understanding where your money makes the biggest impact on sleep quality helps you allocate your budget wisely.

Worth the Splurge: Long-Term Sleep Investments

A handful of bedroom purchases deliver returns that far exceed their price tags by improving comfort night after night for many years. Chief among them is the mattress itself: as earlier chapters emphasized, nothing influences daily well-being more directly. A high-quality mattress that matches your body and sleep style can transform rest for seven to ten years, making it one of the smartest long-term investments you can make. Nearly as important is the pillow that cradles your head and neck. The right height and firmness prevent morning aches, support free breathing, and amplify the benefits of a supportive mattress; while you needn't buy the costliest model, selecting one tailored to your sleep position pays ongoing dividends.

Light control is another area where quality matters. True blackout curtains or shades block stray streetlamps and early dawn light that sabotage melatonin production, helping you slip into deeper stages of sleep. Better fabrics and mechanisms not only darken the room more effectively but also resist warping and fading over time. Beneath the sheets, an unobtrusive mattress protector quietly safeguards your larger investment by sealing out spills, allergens, and dust mites. Modern versions use breathable, waterproof membranes, preserving comfort while prolonging the mattress's lifespan.

Finally, tools that steady your sleeping temperature—whether a quiet fan, a bed-cooling pad, or moisture-wicking performance bedding—address one of the most common causes of nighttime wakings. Because these items act on comfort variables, you feel every single night and typically endure for years, opting for quality over rock-bottom pricing almost always proves the better value.

Smart Savings: Where to Be Frugal

Not every component of a restful bedroom requires a premium price tag. Decorative flourishes—artwork, accent pillows, and small objets d'art—shape mood but never touch your body, so they're prime territory for thrift-store hunts, DIY projects, or sentimental keepsakes that cost little yet feel meaningful. The same pragmatism applies to bed frames. As long as the structure is sturdy and properly supports your mattress, an inexpensive metal platform or a moderately priced wooden frame will perform as a designer showpiece. Think twice before splurging on fad-driven gadgets or fashion-forward duvet prints that may look dated in a year. Trendy items are the easiest way to overspend and under-use.

When it comes to linens, quality still trumps quantity. Two or three well-made sheet sets in rotation give you coverage on laundry day without overflowing the linen closet, whereas a stack of bargain sets often ends up wrinkled and unused. Secondary touches—throw blankets, Euro shams, bedside benches—offer another chance to economize or repurpose pieces you already own. They add visual warmth without dictating sleep quality.

In short, reserve serious investment for the items that make direct, nightly contact with your body—the mattress, pillow, protector, and climate-control tools—while approaching purely aesthetic or replaceable elements with a lighter hand. That balance lets you craft a sanctuary that feels luxurious where it counts and sensible where it doesn't.

Timing Your Purchases Strategically

Stretching your bedroom budget often hinges on buying the right items at the right moment. Apply the same seasonal logic to bedding: scoop up lightweight, summer-ready sheets and quilts in late autumn, and hunt for flannel or heavyweight duvets once spring arrives, when stores are eager to clear out cold-weather stock. January's traditional "white sales" can also yield deep cuts on linens just as household budgets reset for the new year.

If you're comfortable with minor cosmetic wear, don't overlook floor models; a premium mattress or adjustable base that's been gently tested on a showroom floor often sells for hundreds less than its boxed counterpart. Finally, when you do commit to a new mattress, ask about bundle pricing—many retailers will fold in pillows, a mattress protector, or a sheet set at a steep discount, effectively upgrading your entire sleep setup for far less than piece-meal purchases would cost. With a little patience and timing, you can assemble a high-quality sleep environment without overrunning your budget.

The True Cost of Poor Sleep

When considering your sleep investment, remember to factor in the hidden costs of poor sleep:

- Decreased productivity and earning potential
- Higher healthcare costs related to conditions exacerbated by sleep deprivation

- Increased spending on caffeine, energy drinks, and other stimulants
- More frequent illness due to compromised immune function
- Higher risk of accidents and errors that can have financial consequences
- Additional stress on relationships that may require time and resources to repair

These "sleep debt" costs accumulate silently but significantly. When viewed through this lens, investments in better sleep often pay for themselves many times over through improved health, productivity, and quality of life.

Remember Tom, a client I worked with years ago? He balked at spending $1,800 on a new mattress system, seeing it as an extravagance. Six months later, he told me it was "the best money I ever spent." Not only was he sleeping better, but he'd stopped buying energy drinks ($5/day), reduced his headache medication, and was more effective at work—even earning a performance bonus he attributed partly to being more rested and focused. His investment had already paid off.

Creating Your Personal Sleep Sanctuary: Putting It All Together

We've covered a lot of ground in this chapter—from temperature and lighting to decluttering and wise investments. Now, it's time to bring it all together into a practical action plan for transforming your bedroom into a true sleep sanctuary.

Step 1 – Assess Your Current Sleep Environment

Begin with a one-week audit of your nights. Jot down every time you struggle to fall asleep or wake prematurely, and note the likely triggers—street noise, hallway light, an overheating room, an achy shoulder. Record how you feel on rising each morning and watch for patterns. Do you always wake stiff on your left side or groggy whenever the thermostat creeps above 72 °F? If you share a bed, fold your partner's experiences into the log because their comfort (or discomfort) inevitably affects yours. This personal "sleep journal" lets you rank problems by their real-world impact instead of relying on generic advice.

Step 2 – Address the Fundamentals First

Tackle the big levers before fussing with décor. Your mattress comes first; if replacement must wait, experiment with a supportive topper or rotate the bed to an unworn zone. Swap pillows that no longer hold your head in neutral alignment. Solve temperature swings through lighter or heavier bedding, a quiet fan, or a bed-cooling pad. Block intrusive light with blackout curtains and corral devices that emit a blue glow. Finally, tame noise— white-noise machines, soft earplugs, or heavier drapes can muffle everything from traffic to a partner's late-night

Netflix. These foundational tweaks create the baseline on which all other comforts rest.

Step 3 – Declutter Systematically

Now clear the mental and physical congestion that keeps your brain in daytime mode. Remove anything unrelated to sleep or intimacy: unpaid bills, kettlebells, half-folded laundry, even the laptop charger that reminds you of tomorrow's work. Give remaining essentials— clothes, books, skincare—a consistent home so they no longer sprawl across nightstands. Set firm boundaries for electronics: perhaps a charging station outside the doorway and a strict "no work on the bed" rule. Reduce dust traps and improve air quality with occasional deep cleans or an unobtrusive purifier. The aim is a room that feels open enough for your thoughts to settle the moment you cross the threshold.

Step 4 – Add Intentional Comfort

With the basics secure, layer in sensory pleasure. Choose sheets whose fabric delights your skin and whose colors cue calm; add a duvet that invites effort-less temperature tweaks. A throw pillow embroidered by a friend or a framed travel photo can spark quiet joy without cluttering surfaces. If the cent soothes you, keep it subtle—a drop of lavender on the underside of your pillowcase or a tiny diffuser set to shut off after thirty minutes. Swap the overhead glare for bedside lamps that bathe the room in amber during the wind-down time, and keep small comforts—water, lip balm, tissues—within a sleepy arm's reach.

Step 5 – Create Supportive Routines

The room's power is unlocked by how you use it. Adopt an evening ritual—perhaps five minutes of stretching, light reading, or prayer—that begins at the same hour most nights and signals "sleep mode" to your brain. Protect the space by reserving it for rest and intimacy alone, then spend a minute each morning making the bed and a minute each night restoring order; these micro-habits reinforce the sanctuary's identity. As seasons shift, adjust bedding weight, curtain opacity, or humidification so the room keeps pace with environmental change. Finally, practice a moment of gratitude as you lie down—an intentional reminder that this space exists to restore you.

A Sleep Sanctuary in Any Space

These principles scale to any footprint or budget. In a studio apartment, a tall bookshelf or sheer curtain can visually cordon off the bed, while a small rug delineates "sleep territory." Parents sharing a room with a child might use a folding screen and dim-to-red night lights to carve out separate zones. City dwellers combat perpetual din with layered sound masking; renters who can't drill holes hang blackout drapes on tension rods. If funds are tight, prioritize the items that touch your body first—mattress comfort, pillow support, breathable sheets—and upgrade aesthetics gradually. A true sanctuary isn't defined by square footage or designer tags, but by the clear, consistent message it sends: here, you are safe to surrender to deep, nourishing rest.

Your Invitation to Better Rest

Creating a sleep sanctuary isn't a one-time project—it's an ongoing practice of honoring your need for quality rest. As your life changes, your sleep needs may evolve,e too. The key is remaining attentive to how your environment affects your sleep and making adjustments when needed.

Remember Lisa's story from the beginning of this chapter? After making those initial changes to her beautiful but not restful bedroom, she became more attuned to how her environment affected her sleep. When she later moved to a new home, she approached her bedroom design completely differently—starting with sleep support and adding beauty within that framework. The result? A room that was both gorgeous and genuinely restful.

Your sleep sanctuary is a gift you give yourself—a space that honors your need for restoration and supports your well-being in tangible ways. It's worth the attention and care required to create it and the small daily efforts needed to maintain it. Because when you create an environment that truly supports deep, quality sleep, you're not just changing your nights—you're transforming your days as well.

In the next chapter, we'll build on this foundation by exploring the daily rhythms and habits that complement your sleep sanctuary. Because while your sleep environment is crucial, the way you live during your waking hours also profoundly impacts how well you rest at night. Together, these elements create a holistic approach to better sleep that can truly change your life.

7

Sleep Habits and Daily Rhythms

A FEW YEARS ago, I met a man named Mike, who had just retired after a 30-year career in law enforcement. For three decades, Mike had worked rotating shifts—sometimes days, sometimes nights, sometimes weekends. His body clock was, in his words, "completely broken." Now that he finally had the freedom to sleep whenever he wanted, he couldn't sleep at all. He would lie awake until 3 AM, then sleep fitfully until noon, feeling groggy and frustrated. He had the perfect mattress, the perfect pillows, the perfect bedroom setup. But sleep remained elusive.

"I've tried everything," he told me. "Nothing works."

I asked him a simple question: "What time do you go to bed each night?"

He laughed. "Whenever I feel tired. Sometimes 10 PM, sometimes midnight, sometimes later if I'm not sleepy. And I sleep in on weekends to catch up."

This inconsistency was the heart of Mike's problem. After decades of shift work had disrupted his natural rhythms, his body was desperate for consistency—but his fluctuating schedule was making that impossible. His mattress wasn't the issue; his habits were.

After our conversation, Mike made a radical change. He would go to bed at 11 PM and wake up at 7 AM every day—weekdays, weekends, holidays, no exceptions—for one full month. He was skeptical but willing to try anything. Three weeks later, he called me.

"It's working," he said, sounding genuinely surprised. "I'm actually falling asleep. And I'm waking up before my alarm."

Mike's experience highlights a fundamental truth about sleep: even the perfect sleep environment can't overcome poor sleep habits. Your body craves rhythm and routine. It functions best when you honor its natural cycles rather than constantly disrupting them. While your mattress and bedroom create the foundation for good sleep, your daily habits determine whether you can actually access that deep, restorative rest your body needs.

In this chapter, we'll explore how your waking behaviors shape your sleeping experience. We'll dig into the power of consistent routines, the impact of what you eat and drink, the role of exercise, and the importance of creating effective wind-down rituals. Because great sleep doesn't start when your head hits the pillow—it's built throughout your day, one habit at a time.

The Power of Routine: Why Consistent Bedtimes and Wake Times Matter

Your body has an internal clock—called your circadian rhythm—that regulates countless biological processes, including your sleep-wake cycle. This internal timekeeper influences when you feel alert or drowsy, when your body temperature rises and falls, and when various hormones are released. And here's the key insight: this system thrives on predictability.

When you go to bed and wake up at consistent times, your body learns to prepare for sleep and wakefulness at the appropriate moments. Your brain begins releasing melatonin (the sleep hormone) at the right time, your body temperature drops on schedule, and your digestive system adjusts to regular meal times. Everything works in harmony—and sleep becomes easier, deeper, and more restorative.

By contrast, irregular sleep schedules confuse your internal clock. If you go to bed at 10 PM one night, midnight the next, and 11 PM the following night, your brain never knows when to begin sleep preparations. If you sleep until 6 AM on weekdays but noon on weekends, you create what sleep experts call "social jet lag"—essentially forcing your body through the equivalent of multiple time zone changes each week. This inconsistency makes it harder to fall asleep, stay asleep, and wake feeling refreshed.

Creating Your Sleep Schedule

The ideal sleep schedule is one you can maintain seven days a week, including weekends. Here's how to establish a rhythm that works:

1. **Determine your non-negotiable wake time** based on work, family, or other commitments.
2. **Work backward 7-8 hours** (or whatever your optimal sleep duration is) to identify your ideal bedtime.
3. **Commit to this schedule for at least three weeks**—the minimum time needed for your body to adapt to a new rhythm.
4. **Allow a maximum 60-minute variation** on weekends if absolutely necessary, but try to stay as consistent as possible.
5. **Set alarms for both bedtime and waketime** until the rhythm becomes natural.

If you currently have an erratic sleep schedule, don't try to change everything overnight. Shift your bedtime and wake time by 15-30 minutes every few days until you reach your target. Your body will adapt more successfully to gradual changes than to sudden ones.

The Weeknd Reset Myth

One of the most destructive sleep myths is the idea that you can "catch up" on sleep by sleeping in on weekends. This approach actually makes things worse in several ways. It reinforces an irregular circadian rhythm, making weeknight sleep more difficult. It creates Sunday night insomnia as your body resists returning to an earlier schedule. It keeps you in a perpetual state of mild jet lag, affecting mood and cognition. It masks chronic sleep deprivation rather than addressing the root cause.

Instead of using weekends to catch up, use them to maintain the healthy rhythm you've established during the week. If you genuinely need more sleep, it's better to go to bed slightly earlier every night than to dramatically shift your schedule on weekends.

Consistency and Age

As we age, our sensitivity to irregular sleep schedules often increases. Children and teenagers can sometimes bounce back from occasional late nights more easily than adults—though they still benefit enormously from consistent routines. By middle age and beyond, our bodies become less flexible with sleep timing, making consistency even more critical.

This doesn't mean you can never stay out late or sleep in occasionally. Life happens, and rigid adherence to schedules can create its own stress. But it does mean recognizing that consistently honoring your body's need for rhythmic sleep will pay dividends in energy, mood, and overall health—especially as you get older.

Remember Mike, who transformed his sleep by committing to a consistent schedule? Six months after our conversation, he told me he occasionally allows himself a "late night" for special occasions—but his definition of "late" had changed from 2 AM to 11:30 PM, and he still wakes naturally around 7 AM the next day. His body had so fully adapted to its new rhythm that it couldn't go back to its old erratic patterns. And he wouldn't want it to—the improvement in his quality of life was too significant to sacrifice.

Diet and Exercise: How Food Choices, Caffeine, and Workouts Affect Sleep

What you eat, drink, and how you move your body during the day has a profound impact on how well you sleep at night. These daily choices create either the perfect conditions for deep, restorative sleep—or obstacles your body has to overcome before it can truly rest.

Timing Your Meals: When Matters As Much As What

Your digestive system and sleep cycle are intimately connected. Eating too close to bedtime forces your body to focus on digestion when it should be transitioning to sleep. As a general rule, aim to finish your last main meal 2-3 hours before bedtime. This gives your body time to complete most of the digestive process before sleep. If you need a bedtime snack, keep it small and sleep-friendly. Good options include a small piece of fruit with a tablespoon of nut butter, a few whole-grain crackers with cheese, or a small bowl of oatmeal with a sprinkle of cinnamon. These combinations provide slow-releasing energy that helps maintain stable blood sugar throughout the night. Be mindful of dinner composition. Very high-fat meals can take longer to digest and potentially disrupt sleep, while very high-carb meals may initially make you drowsy but could lead to blood sugar fluctuations later in the night.

Food Choices for Better Sleep

Certain foods contain compounds that can help promote better sleep. Tryptophan-rich foods like turkey, chicken, eggs, and dairy contain an amino acid that helps with melatonin production. Magnesium-rich foods such as leafy greens, nuts, seeds, and whole grains help muscles relax and can improve sleep quality. Vitamin B6-rich foods like fish, chickpeas, and bananas help convert tryptophan into melatonin. Potassium-rich foods like bananas, potatoes, and leafy greens can help prevent nighttime leg cramps that disrupt sleep. Calcium-rich foods like dairy products help the brain use tryptophan to produce sleep-inducing melatonin.

While no single food is a sleep miracle worker, a diet rich in whole foods, plenty of vegetables, moderate protein, and healthy fats creates the nutritional foundation for quality sleep.

The Caffeine Connection

Caffeine is a powerful central nervous system stimulant that blocks adenosine—a compound that naturally builds up in your body throughout the day and signals sleepiness. What many people don't realize is how long caffeine remains active in their system:

- The half-life of caffeine (the time it takes for your body to eliminate half of it) is typically 4-6 hours but can be up to 10 hours for some individuals.
- This means that a coffee consumed at 3 PM could be equivalent to drinking a half-cup at 9 PM—right before bed.
- Sensitivity to caffeine increases with age, so the cut-off time that worked in your 20s might cause problems in your 40s and beyond.

For optimal sleep, experiment with gradually earlier caffeine cut-off times until you find what works for you. Many sleep experts recommend avoiding caffeine after 12 PM, but individual sensitivity varies widely. Pay attention to how your body responds, and adjust accordingly.

Hidden Sources of Caffeine

Note that caffeine lurks in many unexpected places. Beyond the obvious coffee, tea, and energy drinks, you'll find it in chocolate (especially dark varieties), some pain relievers and cold medicines, certain flavors of ice cream and yogurt, some weight loss supplements, and many "energy" or "vitamin" waters. Always check labels if you're trying to reduce your caffeine intake, especially in the afternoon and evening.

Alcohol: The Sleep Destroyer

Many people use alcohol as a sleep aid, and it can indeed make falling asleep easier. But this comes at a high cost to sleep quality. Alcohol can disrupt REM sleep, the stage associated with memory consolidation and emotional processing. It increases sleep fragmentation, causing multiple brief awakenings you may not remember. It relaxes throat muscles, potentially worsening snoring and sleep apnea. Acts as a diuretic, increasing middle-of-the-night bathroom trips. And it causes rebound alertness as it metabolizes, often leading to 2-3 AM awakenings.

If you choose to drink alcohol, try to finish your last drink at least 3 hours before bedtime to minimize its impact on your sleep. And be especially careful about combining alcohol with sleep medications—this combination can have dangerous effects beyond just poor sleep quality.

Exercise: Timing Is Everything

Regular physical activity is one of the most powerful sleep promoters available—but timing matters significantly. Morning and early afternoon exercise generally has the most positive effect on that night's sleep. The exertion helps regulate your circadian rhythm, and the post-exercise drop in body temperature several hours later helps signal sleep readiness. Evening exercise works well for some people but can be stimulating for others. If evening is your only option, aim to finish at least 90 minutes before bedtime and consider gentle forms like yoga or stretching rather than intense cardio or heavy strength training. Consistency trumps timing. A regular exercise routine at any time of day is better for sleep than sporadic workouts or no exercise at all. Find what fits your schedule and stick with it.

The type of exercise matters less than its regularity. Walking, swimming, cycling, strength training—all can contribute to better sleep when done consistently. Aim for at least 150 minutes of moderate activity per week, spread across multiple days.

Hydration Balance

Proper hydration supports good sleep, but timing is crucial. Stay well-hydrated throughout the day, especially in the morning and early afternoon. Begin tapering fluid intake about 2 hours before bed to minimize nighttime bathroom trips. If you're waking up thirsty at night, you may be under-hydrated during the day, ay or your bedroom may be too warm.

Remember that many foods (especially fruits and vegetables) contribute to your overall hydration, not just beverages. A balanced approach to hydration throughout the day supports your body's natural sleep processes without creating disruptive bathroom trips.

Screen Time, Stress, and Stimulants: Setting Realistic Limits

In our always-connected world, one of the biggest enemies of quality sleep is the constant stimulation we expose ourselves to right up until bedtime. From scrolling social media to answering late work emails, these activities keep our brains in an alert, activated state—precisely when we should be winding down.

The Blue Light Problem

The screens on our phones, tablets, computers, and TVs emit blue wavelength light that has particularly powerful effects on sleep. Blue light suppresses melatonin production more strongly than other light wavelengths. This suppression can delay sleep onset by 1-3 hours in sensitive individuals. The effect is dose-dependent—more screen time equals more sleep disruption. The impact increases with screen brightness and proximity to your face (making phones and tablets especially problematic)

While many devices now offer "night mode" or blue light filters, these only reduce, not eliminate, the problematic light. The content itself—whether it's work emails, news headlines, or social media—can be mentally stimulating regardless of the color temperature of the screen.

Digital Boundaries for Better Sleep

You don't have to exile every gadget from your life to protect your sleep, but you do need firm boundaries. Begin with a nightly "screen curfew." Power down phones, tablets, and laptops at least 30–60 minutes before lights out so your brain can detach from alerts, blue light, and mental stimulation. Make that easier by parking devices in a charging station outside the bedroom; when your phone isn't glowing on the nightstand, the urge to scroll fades. Replace its wake-up duty with an old-fashioned alarm clock, removing the temptation to sneak one last glance at messages right before you nod off—or the moment you open your eyes.

Technology itself can help enforce limits. Many phones allow you to schedule app blocks or grayscale modes that dull the appeal of social feeds as bedtime nears. If evening screen time is unavoidable—perhaps you're finishing a project or watching a show—engage a blue-light filter and dial brightness down to the lowest comfortable setting. Remember, this is progress, not perfection. Trimming just 15–30 minutes of pre-sleep screen exposure can noticeably improve how quickly you drift off and how refreshed you feel in the morning.

The Stress-Sleep Cycle

Stress and sleep play a tug-of-war with each other. A restless night amplifies anxiety hormones the next day, while an overloaded mind sabotages the very best that could restore it. The first step to breaking this loop is drawing a bright line between work and repose. If you work from home, physically close the laptop, power down the monitor, and—if possible—shut the door on your workspace at a consistent hour so your brain can stop scanning for emails and start preparing for evening calm.

Before you launch your wind-down routine, give your worries a safe holding tank. Spend ten focused minutes jotting down loose ends—unfinished tasks, nagging concerns, anything that keeps mental gears grinding—and then literally close the notebook. This simple "worry download" assures your mind the issues are captured and can wait until tomorrow.

Next, create a mental off-ramp that shifts you from daytime vigilance to nighttime ease. It might be a short walk around the block, a warm shower, a few pages of light reading, or gentle stretches set to soft music. Over time, that ritual becomes a neural cue: daylight concerns off, restorative mode on. Reinforce the transition by steering clear of evening triggers—doom-scrolling the news, bingeing adrenaline-pumping shows, or diving into heated discussions that spike cortisol right when your body should be dialing it down.

Life will deliver seasons—new parenthood, looming deadlines, family illness—when stress is non-negotiable. In those periods, meticulous sleep hygiene is a lifeline, not a luxury. Safeguard consistent bedtimes, keep the bedroom cool and dark, and double down on the boundaries and rituals that tell your nervous system it is safe to stand down. High stress doesn't doom you to sleepless nights, but it does demand deliberate strategies that give rest a fighting chance.

Hidden Stimulants Beyond Caffeine

Caffeine isn't the only hidden saboteur of a good night's sleep. Nicotine is a potent stimulant, too; smoking or vaping within two to three hours of bedtime can delay sleep onset and fragment the night with micro-awakenings. Certain over-the-counter and prescription drugs also contain stimulating ingredients. Decongestants, weight-control aids, and some combination pain relievers, for example, can elevate heart rate and keep the brain on high alert long after lights out, so ask your pharmacist or physician whether shifting the dose to earlier in the day might help. Even a seemingly harmless evening treat can backfire: sugar-heavy snacks and refined carbohydrates spike blood glucose, then trigger a crash that may jolt you awake. Pair late-night nibbles with protein or healthy fats to keep blood sugar—and sleep—stable. Herbal products marketed for "energy," "focus," or "metabolism" can be equally problematic. Many teas, capsules, and powdered supplements hide natural stimulants that linger into bedtime, so read labels closely if you use them after lunch. And remember: never adjust prescribed medications or long-standing supplements on your own. Consult your healthcare provider first; protecting sleep is crucial, but so is maintaining the therapeutic intent of your treatment plan.

Wind-Down Rituals: Relaxation Techniques That Work

The transition from daytime activity to nighttime rest doesn't happen automatically—especially in our stimulation-rich modern environment. Your brain and body need clear signals that it's time to shift gears. This is where wind-down rituals become essential.

A wind-down ritual is a consistent series of calming activities that helps your brain recognize that sleep is approaching. Over time, these rituals become powerful sleep cues that can actually begin to trigger your natural sleep responses. Think of them as a bridge between your busy day and your restful night.

Bedtime rituals work because the brain craves predictable signals that it can file under "safe to power down." When you perform the same soothing sequence every night, the routine dampens the vigilance systems that keep you alert, nudges the nervous system from fight-or-flight into rest-and-digest, and steadily lowers stress hormones such as cortisol. Over time, the activities themselves become conditioned cues: your brain recognizes the pattern and begins secreting sleep-promoting neurochemicals even before you climb under the covers. Studies consistently show that people who follow an established wind-down routine fall asleep faster and wake less often than those with ad-hoc habits—the exact steps matter far less than their calm nature and unwavering consistency.

An effective wind-down spans roughly thirty to sixty minutes and unfolds in the same order each night. It begins with a clear transition signal that tells your body the workday is finished: slipping into soft evening clothes, washing your face, dimming overhead lights in favor of amber lamplight, queuing a playlist you reserve for this hour, or sipping a mug of caffeine-free tea. These modest gestures act like a porchlight that guides your circadian rhythm toward the front door of sleep.

Next come elements that relax the body itself. Gentle stretching can ease knots in the neck, shoulders, and lower back. A slow pass with a foam roller or massage ball further melts residual tension. A warm shower—or better yet, a fifteen-minute soak—warms the core and then allows it to cool, mimicking the natural temperature drop that precedes sleep. Progressive muscle relaxation or a few minutes of 4-7-8 breathing slows the heart rate and deepens respiration, helping every system throttle down.

With muscles unwound, turn to the mind. Choose quiet, absorbing activities that occupy just enough attention to crowd out rumination without revving you up: a chapter of light fiction, a narrated "sleep story," a gratitude journal entry, a brief meditation, or even a gentle crossword if puzzles soothe rather than frustrate you. The goal is mental idling, not problem-solving.

The environment keeps pace with these internal shifts. Lights dim further until only a bedside glow remains. Phones go silent or stay outside the room, while a soft white-noise track or rustling leaves app masks random disturbances. Lower the thermostat a couple of degrees, adjust bedding, and, if you enjoy scent cues, let a whisper of lavender or cedar drift from a diffuser set to shut off automatically.

The true power of any wind-down lies in its repeatability. Follow the same sequence whenever possible, even when you travel; portable anchors such as an e-reader, a stretch strap, or a familiar playlist help recreate the routine in new spaces. If time runs short, keep the core moves but compress them rather than substituting stimulating activities. Most people notice that within two or three weeks of steady practice, sleepiness arrives on cue, making the glide into slumber smoother and more reliable.

Sharing a bedroom adds another layer of choreography. Partners with different preferences can designate part of the home as a quiet zone after a certain hour, rely on headphones for mismatched audio tastes, or stagger lights-out times so each person gets the ritual they need. Joint wind-down activities—perhaps reading side by side or doing synchronized stretches—can even deepen connection while promoting better rest. With clear communication and a dash of creativity, two distinct evening rhythms can harmonize rather than clash, ensuring that each sleeper's brain receives the calm, consistent signals it needs to let go of the day.

Putting It All Together: Your 24-Hour Sleep Success Plan

Sleep isn't just a nighttime activity—it's influenced by choices you make throughout your entire day. To truly transform your rest, you need a holistic approach that aligns your daily rhythm with your body's natural sleep cycles. Here's what a sleep-supporting day looks like from morning to night:

Morning — Setting the Stage

The day's first hour quietly programs the night to come. Wake at roughly the same time every morning—weekday or weekend—to keep the internal clock ticking in rhythm. Step outside or at least stand by a bright window for ten to fifteen minutes of natural light; those photons reset the brain's master timekeeper and anchor your circadian schedule. Breakfast should be steady, not spike: pair complex carbs with protein and healthy fats so blood-sugar levels cruise instead of crashing by mid-morning. Finally, move a little. A brisk walk with the dog, a few sun salutations, and even vigorous house-tidying tells every cell, "We're awake," making it easier for sleep pressure to build at the proper pace through the day.

Daytime — Maintaining Energy Balance

What you do between breakfast and dinner determines whether bedtime feels like a welcome descent or an uphill slog. Keep caffeine strategic: enjoy your last cup no later than mid-afternoon—about eight to ten hours before lights out—to avoid lingering stimulation. Eat meals on a reasonably consistent timetable. Erratic grazing followed by giant catch-up meals whipsaw energy and hormones. Thread physical activity into the day—a lunchtime walk, stair breaks, brief stretch sessions—to accumulate the movement that deepens the nighttime sleep drive. If you work under artificial light, slip outside for brief daylight hits to reinforce circadian signals, and hydrate steadily while tapering liquids in the late evening so midnight bathroom trips don't break your cycles.

Evening — The Transition Phase

As sunset approaches, nudge your body and mind toward slower gears. Finish dinner two or three hours before bed, giving digestion a head start. Swap bright overhead bulbs for warm, low lamps; declining light cues melatonin release and a gentle drop in core temperature. A slightly cooler room furthers that signal. Shutdown work with a brief "closing ritual"— jot tomorrow's top tasks, power down devices, and physically close the laptop—so lingering to-dos don't trail you into the bedroom. Begin replacing screens and intense entertainment with quieter, less stimulating pastimes.

Before Bed — The Wind-Down Window

The final sixty minutes form a protective buffer. Follow a consistent ritual—perhaps changing into sleep-only clothes, brewing an herbal tea, reading a chapter of fiction, then doing five minutes of gentle stretches. Dim lights to their lowest setting, set room temperature, cue white noise if helpful, and confirm devices are silenced or charging elsewhere. When worries intrude, deposit them on paper for tomorrow's attention, then close the notebook. End the ritual by noting a few gratitudes. This positive framing lowers arousal and invites peace.

Bedtime — The Final Transition

Aim to crawl under the covers at roughly the same hour each night, responding to genuine sleepiness cues such as drooping eyelids and slowed thinking. Abandon any urge to "force" sleep; instead, adopt a mindset of rest-fulness—allowing rather than chasing slumber. Arrange your body so the spine feels neutral limbs loose. If thoughts flare, redirect attention to the rhythm of your breath or a calming image instead of following stimu-lating mental threads.

When the Unexpected Happens

Life isn't always predictable, and sometimes disrup-tions to your ideal sleep routine are unavoidable. When this happens:

- **Return to your core habits** as soon as possible rather than extending the disruption
- **Be gentle with yourself** rather than stressing about one imperfect night
- **Focus on what you can control** even when some elements are beyond your influence
- **Remember that consistency over time** matters more than perfection every single day
- **Use sleep disruptions as information** about what affects your rest, not as failures

With a solid foundation of good sleep habits, your body becomes more resilient—able to return to balanced sleep more quickly after inevitable disruptions.

The Cumulative Effect

The beauty of this 24-hour approach to sleep is that it works with your body's natural processes rather than fighting them. Each sleep-supporting habit reinforces the others, creating an upward spiral of better rest and greater energy. While changing everything at once can feel overwhelming, even small adjustments—implemented consistently—can begin to improve your sleep quality.

Remember Mike from the beginning of this chapter? The man who transformed his sleep by establishing a consistent schedule after retirement? His success didn't come from changing everything overnight. He started with consistent wake and bedtimes, then gradually added other supportive habits—morning walks, an evening reading ritual, and limits on late-day caffeine. Each change built upon the previous ones, eventually creating a complete rhythm that supported deep, restorative sleep.

Your path might look different, but the principle remains the same: sleep thrives on rhythm. When you align your daily habits with your body's natural cycles, you create the conditions for the kind of rest that truly restores body, mind, and spirit. And while it takes some effort to establish these patterns, the rewards—greater energy, clearer thinking, more stable mood, and improved overall health—are more than worth it.

In our next chapter, we'll tackle the common sleep challenges that can disrupt even the best habits and environments. From stress and anxiety to physical pain and shift work, we'll explore practical strategies for overcoming these obstacles and finding your way back to restful sleep.

8

Overcoming Common
Sleep Struggles

A WOMAN NAMED Rachel visited one of my stores last year. She was in her mid-forties, successful, intelligent, and, by all external measures, thriving. But her tired eyes told another story. As we talked about mattresses, she suddenly paused and looked at me with unexpected vulnerability.

"I don't know if a new mattress will even help," she admitted. "I haven't had a good night's sleep in over two years. My mind just won't shut off. I lie there thinking about work, my kids, my parents' health... everything. Sometimes, I'm still awake at 3 AM, and then I panic about how tired I'll be the next day, which makes it even worse."

Rachel's struggle is painfully common. Even with the perfect mattress, ideal sleep environment, and solid daily habits, many people face specific obstacles that keep quality sleep just out of reach. While the foundations we've covered in previous chapters are essential, sometimes we need targeted strategies for particular challenges.

In this chapter, we'll address the most common sleep disruptors—stress and anxiety, physical pain, breathing issues like snoring and sleep apnea, and the complex challenges of shift work and travel. These aren't just occasional inconveniences; they're significant barriers that can turn sleep from something restful into something stressful. But they don't have to be permanent roadblocks. With the right approach, even long-standing sleep struggles can be overcome.

I'm not a doctor, and the strategies in this chapter don't replace appropriate medical care. Some sleep issues require professional intervention, and I'll help you recognize when to seek that help. But many sleep challenges can be significantly improved with targeted self-care strategies—and that's what we'll focus on here. Let's dive into these common struggles and how to address them, starting with the one that affects more people than perhaps any other: the racing mind that just won't quiet down when it's time to rest.

Stress and Anxiety: Mindset Shifts, Breathing Exercises, and Journaling Approaches

When Rachel told me about her racing thoughts at bedtime, I recognized a pattern I've seen hundreds of times. Mental activation—whether from stress, anxiety or simply an active mind—is one of the most common obstacles to restful sleep. Your body might be ready for sleep, but your mind keeps running, analyzing the day behind you or planning for the day ahead, refusing to shift into its natural rest state.

This isn't just frustrating; it creates a vicious cycle. The more you worry about not sleeping, the more alert you become. The more alert you become, the harder it is to sleep. And the harder it is to sleep, the more you worry. Breaking this cycle requires both practical techniques and a fundamental shift in how you think about sleep itself.

The Paradox of Sleep Effort

Here's a strange truth about sleep: the harder you try to make it happen, the more elusive it becomes. Sleep isn't something you do; it's something you allow. It's a natural biological process that occurs when you create the right conditions and then get out of its way. This insight—that you can't force sleep but can only invite it—is transformative for many people caught in the stress-sleep cycle.

When you lie in bed thinking, "I must fall asleep right now," you're actually activating your brain rather than relaxing it. You're triggering performance anxiety and creating mental pressure that works against your body's natural sleep mechanisms. The shift from "trying to sleep" to "allowing sleep" might seem subtle, but it can make a profound difference in how quickly and easily you drift off.

Practical Strategies for the Racing Mind

For Rachel and others whose thoughts seem to accelerate at bedtime, these practical approaches can help quiet the mental chatter:

The "Worry Journal" Technique

Set aside 15 minutes before your wind-down routine (not in bed) to transfer racing thoughts from your mind to paper. Write down everything that's on your mind—tasks, concerns, ideas, problems. For each worry, jot down one small next step you could take tomorrow. Symbolically "close" your worry time by literally closing the journal. If thoughts resurface in bed, gently remind yourself, "I've captured that, and I'll handle it tomorrow."

This practice helps your brain recognize that concerns have been acknowledged and temporarily addressed, making it easier to let them go until morning.

Body-Based Calming Techniques

When anxiety surges, and your body slips into a racing-heart, shallow-breath state, the fastest way back to calm is often through physical techniques that speak directly to the nervous system. A simple but powerful tool is **4-7-8 breathing**: inhale through your nose for a slow count of four, hold that breath for seven counts, then exhale through pursed lips for eight. The prolonged exhalation lengthens vagal tone, nudging the parasympathetic nervous system into gear and telling the body it is safe. You can reinforce that message with a **progressive body scan**: start at your toes, consciously soften each muscle group, and work methodically upward until your brow and jaw unclench. Many people also swear by the steady, cocoon-like pressure of a **weighted blanket**— ideally about ten percent of body weight—which mimics deep-touch therapy and lowers physiological arousal enough to ease the mind toward sleep.

When to Seek Help for Sleep Anxiety

While the strategies above help many people, persistent insomnia sometimes requires additional support:

- **Cognitive Behavioral Therapy for Insomnia (CBT-I)** is highly effective for anxiety-related sleep problems and is usually the first treatment recommended by sleep specialists.
- **If anxiety is affecting multiple areas of your life** beyond just sleep, working with a mental health professional can address the root causes.
- **When sleep problems persist for more than a month** despite consistent sleep hygiene practices, consult with a healthcare provider to rule out underlying conditions.
- **If panic attacks or severe anxiety occur at bedtime**, professional support can provide more intensive strategies and, if appropriate, medication options.

Remember Rachel from the beginning of this section? After implementing a worry journal practice, setting an earlier bedtime to reduce sleep pressure, and learning the 4-7-8 breathing technique, she reported significant improvement within three weeks. "I still have bad nights sometimes," she told me, "but they're the exception now, not the rule. And I don't panic about them anymore, which makes a huge difference."

Pain Management: How to Adapt Your Sleep Environment

Physical pain presents a particularly challenging sleep obstacle because it creates a frustrating cycle. Pain disrupts sleep, and poor sleep often increases pain sensitivity. Whether you're dealing with chronic conditions like arthritis or fibromyalgia, recovering from an injury or surgery, or simply experiencing the normal aches that can come with aging, finding ways to minimize pain during the night is essential for restorative sleep.

Understanding Pain and Sleep

The relationship between pain and sleep is bidirectional. Pain makes it difficult to find comfortable sleeping positions and can cause frequent awakenings. Sleep deprivation lowers pain thresholds, making existing pain feel more intense. Poor sleep reduces the body's natural pain control mechanisms. The stress of managing pain can itself contribute to sleep difficulties.

Breaking this cycle usually requires addressing both sides of the equation: finding ways to minimize pain's impact on sleep while also ensuring that sleep quality is optimized to support the body's pain management capabilities.

Mattress Solutions for Different Pain Conditions

When chronic pain is part of the picture, your mattress becomes less of a piece of furniture, and more of a therapeutic tool, and the right choice depends on where you hurt. For persistent lower-back pain, most studies converge on a medium-firm feel that supports the lumbar curve without letting the pelvis sink. Mattresses with zoned construction—slightly softer under the shoulders, extra reinforcement beneath the waist and hips—can fine-tune that balance, while memory foam or latex layers add contouring that hugs the spine yet prevents hammocking.

Side sleepers battling hip or shoulder pain usually need a touch more softness in the comfort layer so those joints don't bear the night's full weight. Again, high-density memory foam and supple latex excel because they spread pressure evenly while a supportive core keeps alignment intact. Some manufacturers now build targeted relief channels or cut-outs beneath the shoulder and hip zones; if joint pain is your main complaint, those designs are worth a test.

Patients with systemic conditions like arthritis or fibromyalgia face additional hurdles. Overheating can amplify pain sensitivity, and any mattress that resists movement makes nighttime position changes exhausting. Look for breathable hybrids or quick-response foams that contour without trapping heat, and consider adjustable-air beds whose firmness can be tweaked day-to-day as symptoms flare or ease.

Neck pain shifts the spotlight to your pillow, though the mattress still matters in keeping the upper spine level. Choose a pillow matched to your primary sleep posture—higher and firmer for side sleeping, lower for back, nearly flat for stomach—so the cervical vertebrae remain in neutral alignment. Cervical-contour memory foam models, adjustable water pillows, or hybrid fills that mold to the exact curve of your neck often provide the most consistent relief.

Because pain is deeply individual, what soothes one body may irritate another, even with identical diagnoses. Approach any new sleep surface as an experiment: give yourself several weeks for muscles and joints to adapt, track how you feel on waking, and be ready to fine-tune or exchange components until the bed actively supports rather than aggravates your recovery.

Optimizing Your Sleep Position

Your sleeping posture can either soothe or aggravate pain, so small adjustments often deliver outsized relief.

Back sleepers benefit from sliding a thin pillow beneath the knees. The slight elevation eases the lumbar curve and unloads pressure on the lower spine. Pair that with a head pillow high enough to support the natural neck curve but not so thick that it juts the chin toward the chest. If your mattress lacks mid-back support, a slim lumbar roll tucked beneath the small of the back can help.

Keep arms by your sides or rest lightly on the abdomen—lifting them overhead stresses the shoulder capsule and may provoke tingling or morning stiffness.

Side sleepers should insert a firm pillow between the knees to stop the top leg from rotating the hips and pulling the spine out of line. The main head pillow must fill the shoulder-to-ear gap so the neck stays level; too little loft tilts the head downward, while too much kinks it upward. A full-length body pillow can cradle the upper arm and nestle between the knees at once, maintaining alignment from shoulders to ankles. If one hip or shoulder grows tender, alternate sides rather than settling night after night on the same one.

Stomach sleeping poses the steepest biomechanical challenges because it hyper-extends the lower back and twists the neck. Transitioning to the side or back is ideal, but if prone is the only position that feels natural, slip a slender pillow—or a folded towel—under the hips to flatten lumbar arching and use an ultra-flat head pillow (or none at all) to limit neck rotation. Some people hug a body pillow to start retraining themselves toward a side-lying posture without feeling confined.

Combination sleepers—those who shift among positions—need a mattress and bedding that accommodate motion without resistance. Responsive foams or hybrid surfaces make turning easier, and adjustable bases let you fine-tune angles that ease different pain points. Keep versatile pillows nearby: one lofty enough for side sleeping and a slimmer backup for the moments you roll onto your back or stomach. By shaping your support to each posture, you prevent localized stress and wake with less pain, no matter how much you roam across the mattress at night.

Beyond the Mattress: Additional Pain Management Strategies

A supportive mattress and pillow set the stage for pain-free rest, but several adjunct practices can make the difference between a merely tolerable night and a genuinely restorative one. Temperature therapy is a versatile first line of relief. Applying gentle heat—whether through a warm bath, a microwaveable heat pack, or a pre-warmed bed—loosens tight muscles and boosts blood flow to chronically sore areas. Conversely, a cool gel pack or chilled compress can calm inflammatory flare-ups or fresh injuries. Some specialty pillows now offer built-in heating or cooling elements for pinpoint comfort, though it is best to avoid sleeping all night on an electric pad; use heat to prepare the body for bed, then remove the device before dozing off.

Light movement in the hour before bedtime further tempers discomfort. A brief routine of targeted stretches or sleep-focused yoga poses relieves residual tension, while daytime water exercise builds strength with minimal joint impact, often translating into fewer nocturnal aches. Because every pain profile is unique, a physical therapist can tailor a pre-sleep sequence that protects vulnerable joints without over-straining them.

Medication timing also matters. If you take analgesics, consult your doctor about scheduling doses so the peak effect coincides with your usual bedtime. Some pain drugs, particularly opioids, can disrupt sleep architecture, so complementing or partially replacing them with non-pharmacological strategies—heat, cold, relaxation training—may improve both pain control and sleep quality. Always raise sleep concerns with the prescriber. Dosage or formulation adjustments are sometimes possible.

Because pain intensifies under stress, relaxation techniques become doubly valuable. Progressive muscle relaxation can be modified to avoid over-contracting sensitive areas, while mindfulness or acceptance-based meditation trains the mind to observe pain sensations without escalating anxiety. Guided imagery scripts that focus on easing pain signals gently usher the nervous system toward a sleep-ready state.

For certain conditions, mechanical support offers final fine-tuning. Adjustable bed bases let you elevate knees, head, or both to unload spinal pressure, and wedges or bolsters can cradle a post-surgery limb or keep acid reflux in check. A high-quality mattress topper may soften an overly firm bed or add stability to one that has begun to sag, all without the expense of a full replacement.

Self-care, however, has limits. Seek professional help if pain wakes you repeatedly despite these measures, if fear of nighttime discomfort leads you to dread or avoid sleep, or if daytime function is eroding. Worsening or qualitatively changing pain and reliance on alcohol or sedatives to force sleep also signal the need for expert evaluation. A combined approach—drawing on insights from both pain and sleep specialists—often yields the most effective, sustainable relief.

A client named Robert came to me with severe arthritic hip pain that had made good sleep impossible for over a year. We found him a pressure-relieving mattress with zoned support, but what really transformed his sleep was the complete system: the right mattress, a between-the-knees pillow, an evening gentle yoga routine, and timing his medication optimally for sleep. No single element solved the problem, but the combination finally broke his pain-sleep cycle. That's often how it works—not one magic solution, but a thoughtful approach addressing multiple aspects of the challenge.

Snoring and Sleep Apnea: When to See a Specialist

Breathing issues during sleep affect millions of people, ranging from occasional mild snoring to severe sleep apnea, which can have serious health consequences. While not everyone who snores has sleep apnea, and not all sleep apnea causes noticeable snoring, these issues share a common theme: disrupted breathing that prevents truly restorative sleep.

Understanding Snoring and Sleep Apnea

Snoring occurs when air can't move freely through your nose and throat during sleep, causing the surrounding tissues to vibrate and create that familiar sound. It can be caused by many factors, including:

- Relaxed throat muscles (often intensified by alcohol, certain medications, or deep sleep)
- Anatomical features like enlarged tonsils or a deviated septum
- Nasal congestion from allergies or infections
- Weight gain that increases tissue around the airway
- Aging, which naturally relaxes throat muscles
- Sleep position, particularly back sleeping, which allows the tongue to fall backward.

While occasional light snoring is generally harmless, heavy chronic snoring often signals a problem that deserves attention—both for the snorer's sleep quality and for their bed partners.

Sleep apnea is more serious and involves actual pauses in breathing during sleep. With obstructive sleep apnea (the most common form), the airway repeatedly becomes partially or completely blocked during sleep, causing breathing to stop briefly—sometimes dozens or even hundreds of times per night. When the brain registers the oxygen drop, it briefly wakes you to restore normal breathing, though these awakenings are often so brief you don't remember them.

Warning Signs That Require Medical Attention

The breathing difficulties discussed in these pages can't always be solved with do-it-yourself measures. Some warrant a thorough medical evaluation. Schedule an appointment if your partner complains of loud, disruptive snoring or if anyone has noticed that you stop breathing for stretches while asleep. Red flags also include abrupt awakenings with a gasp or choking sensation, unrelenting daytime sleepiness despite spending enough hours in bed, and morning headaches that lift only after you've been up for a while. Many people with sleep-disordered breathing struggle to focus, find their mood sagging into unexplained irritability or depression, or wake each day with an unusually dry mouth or sore throat. Persistently high blood pressure that resists usual treatment can be another clue. These symptoms often point to obstructive sleep apnea, a condition tied to elevated risks of heart disease, stroke, type 2 diabetes, and traffic accidents caused by drowsy driving. Because the stakes are so high, proper diagnosis—typically a sleep study—and evidence-based treatment are essential rather than optional.

The Role of Your Mattress and Sleep Environment

Although a mattress itself can't treat sleep apnea, the way you set up your bed can make breathing therapies far more effective. An adjustable base that lets you raise the head of the bed even a modest amount relies on gravity to keep the upper airway from collapsing, which often softens snoring and lightens apnea episodes. If you use CPAP, specialty pillows with cut-outs or contours for the mask and hose prevent dislodging the equipment when you turn over, boosting comfort and long-term compliance. Because side sleeping tends to reduce airway obstruction compared with lying flat on your back, choose a mattress—and perhaps a body pillow—that supports that posture without pressuring the shoulders or hips. Allergy sufferers should invest in hypoallergenic covers and washable bedding to minimize overnight congestion that can narrow air passages, and everyone using pressurized air benefits from gentle humidification in the bedroom to keep nasal tissues from drying out. Put together, these tweaks create a sleep environment that works with—rather than against—the therapies that keep you breathing freely through the night.

Living and Sleeping Well with CPAP

Adapting to continuous positive airway pressure (CPAP) therapy can feel awkward at first, but nearly everyone who sticks with it reports dramatic improvements in daytime energy, mood, and overall health. Give yourself permission to ease in; most people need several nights—sometimes weeks—to stop noticing the equipment. Your sleep specialist is your ally here, adjusting mask style and size until it fits both your face and your preferred sleep position. On many machines, the "ramp" setting starts the airflow at a lower pressure and gradually increases it as you drift off, making the transition far less jarring. A heated humidifier attachment can head off the dry mouth and nasal irritation that discourage so many newcomers. Cleanliness matters, too: a brief, consistent routine of rinsing, air-drying, and occasional deep cleaning keeps the device fresh and performing properly. Some people swap their regular pillows for models contoured to cradle CPAP masks and hoses so nothing shifts when they roll over. For extra motivation, online forums and local support groups let you trade hacks and celebrate milestones with others on the same journey. I've watched countless skeptics turn into enthusiasts; James, a long-haul trucker who once browsed mattresses in my store, told me later, "My CPAP saved my marriage and probably my life. The first week was miserable, but now I'd never go back—I feel like a different person every day."

Of course, untreated snoring doesn't just rob the snorer of rest—it echoes through the room and steals sleep from anyone sharing the bed. If your partner's log-sawing is sabotaging your nights, remember that separate sleeping arrangements can be a relationship-preserving, not relationship-ending, choice; well-rested couples are kinder couples. In the meantime, white-noise machines, box fans, or sleep-friendly noise-canceling earbuds can drown out the racket. Approach the issue as a shared health concern rather than a mere annoyance: habitual, loud snoring often signals obstructive sleep apnea or another medical problem that deserves treatment. Some partners even reset their own schedules, turning in a little earlier so they're already in deeper, harder-to-disturb sleep stages before the snoring begins. However you handle it, keep the larger goal in focus:

resolving snoring improves the sleeper's cardiovascular and cognitive health and restores peace to the bedroom for both of you.

Travel and Shift Work: Adapting Your Sleep Strategies

When your schedule changes regularly due to work demands or travel across time zones, your body's natural sleep-wake cycle faces significant challenges. While perfect sleep may not be possible in these situations, strategic approaches can minimize disruption and help you get the most restorative rest possible under challenging circumstances.

The Challenge of Shift Work

Working nights or rotating through different shifts forces the body to live out of sync with its built-in circadian rhythm. When that mismatch is chronic, many people develop Shift Work Sleep Disorder, a condition marked by insomnia, unrelenting daytime (or nighttime) sleepiness, dips in performance, and a higher risk of errors or accidents. Although you can't erase the biological strain entirely, you can blunt its impact with a disciplined approach to sleep, light, and lifestyle.

If you work a permanent night schedule, begin by anchoring your days with a consistent sleep window— even on your days off, if social life allows. A regular "bedtime," whether it falls at 8 a.m. or noon, gives your internal clock a fighting chance to stabilize. Turn the bedroom into a bona fide sleep cave: blackout curtains or an eye mask to banish daylight, a white-noise machine or earplugs to muffle daytime sounds, and a slightly cool temperature to mimic the body's natural drop in core heat. Pair that environment with tactical light use. Soak up bright, blue-rich light during the overnight shift to stay alert, slip on dark sunglasses for the commute home, and keep lights dim—or use amber bulbs—during the hour before crawling into bed. Some shift workers add a low-dose melatonin supplement before their daytime sleep; do this only under medical guidance, as timing and dosage are crucial.

Sleep block protection also requires social and behavioral boundaries. Let family and friends know your "off-duty" hours, silence the phone, and post a schedule on the fridge so no one forgets. Because your biology already runs uphill, tighten your sleep hygiene. Skip caffeine late in the shift, steer clear of alcohol before bed, and eat on a regular timetable that matches your altered day so appetite rhythms don't work against your sleep drive.

Rotating shifts complicate matters further, yet you can still soften the blow. Whenever possible, lobby for forward-rotating schedules that progress from mornings to evenings to nights. The brain adapts more easily to that direction than backward rotation. Try to build a buffer day between shift changes, or at least start nudging your sleep and meal times one to two hours toward the new schedule in the days just before the switch. A brief nap—either in the late afternoon before a first night shift or during an approved break—can erase enough sleep debt to keep you functioning. Use caffeine sparingly and early in the shift so it doesn't linger when it's time to sleep. Finally, accept that seamless adaptation is unlikely when your timetable keeps changing. Concentrate instead on protecting the quality of whatever sleep you can secure, recognizing that small, consistent habits yield the biggest dividends over time.

Navigating Travel and Jet Lag

Leaping across time zones scrambles your body's internal clock, often leaving you with the cluster of symptoms known as jet lag—fatigue, erratic sleep, digestive upset, fuzzy thinking, and mood swings. How hard it hits usually depends on the number of time zones crossed and the direction of travel; flying east tends to be tougher on circadian rhythms than heading west.

Mitigation begins before you board the plane. In the three or four days leading up to departure, start nudging your schedule toward the destination's clock by shifting meals and bedtimes one to two hours earlier or later each day. Enter the trip well-rested because beginning the journey with a sleep debt only magnifies jet lag fatigue. If you have some flexibility, book flights that land in the early evening; that timing makes it easier to stay awake until a sensible local bedtime.

While in transit, protect your future self by staying hydrated and going easy on alcohol and caffeinated drinks, both of which intensify dehydration and fracture sleep. If the flight overlaps with what would normally be your nighttime at home, a brief nap can help, but keep it short unless the snooze aligns with the destination's dark hours. Create a sleep-friendly bubble on board—earplugs, an eye mask, and noise-canceling headphones block the sensory clutter—and get up to stretch every couple of hours to keep blood flowing and joints limber.

The real reset starts the moment you land. Commit immediately to the local timetable for eating, sleeping, and activity, even if your body protests. Seek bright morning sunlight—ideally within the first hour after waking—because natural light is the strongest cue for resetting circadian rhythms. If exhaustion becomes overwhelming, a 20- to 30-minute nap can take the edge off, but avoid long daytime sleep that will push bedtime later. Limit caffeine to the first part of the local morning so it doesn't sabotage your new nighttime. Finally, some travelers find that a small dose of melatonin, taken under a healthcare provider's guidance, signals the brain that it's time to sleep according to the new clock. Combined, these strategies help your body sync faster, letting you enjoy—and remember—your time on the ground.

Creating Sleep Opportunities in Challenging Environments

Getting consistent, restorative rest when you're away from home can be tricky, but you can stack the odds in your favor by treating any unfamiliar bedroom as a makeshift "sleep zone." Start by assembling a portable sleep kit before you leave. An eye mask that blocks light completely, a set of high-quality earplugs or noise-canceling earbuds, and either a white-noise app on your phone or a pocket-sized sound machine will insulate you from the most common hotel or guest-room disruptions. Add a travel pillow suited to your sleep position, a light, breathable blanket for unpredictable thermostats, and a small vial of an essential oil scent you already associated with bedtime; these familiar cues tell your nervous system it's safe to power down.

Once you arrive, turn the room itself into friendlier territory. Drape a T-shirt or piece of tape over blinking LEDs, slide a rolled towel along the base of the door to block hallway light, and, if you can't adjust the thermostat, ask for a different room or bring the temperature down with a fan. Don't hesitate to nudge furniture around so your bed faces away from bright windows, and pinch hotel-hanger clips onto the curtain edges when they refuse to meet in the middle.

Finally, protect the rhythms your body already knows. Pack one or two small bedside objects from home—a favorite paperback, a photo, even your own mug for herbal tea—so the setting feels less foreign. Go through the same wind-down ritual you practice at home, whether that's deep breathing, light stretching, or a brief prayer, and queue up the same sleep-story app or ambient playlist you normally use. Most importantly, keep your target bedtime and wake-up time consistent; when the clock stays predictable, your circadian rhythm can shrug off almost any unfamiliar surroundings.

The Reality Check: Managing Expectations

With both shift work and travel, it's important to have realistic expectations. Your body evolved with a strong connection to natural light-dark cycles, and working against these natural rhythms comes with inevitable challenges. Rather than striving for perfect sleep in these situations, focus on:

- Getting the best sleep possible under the circumstances
- Maximizing sleep quality even when ideal quantity isn't possible
- Recovering strategically when you return to a more normal schedule
- Using strategic naps to supplement when full sleep isn't achievable
- Recognizing the temporary nature of travel disruptions or particular shift assignments

This realistic approach reduces the anxiety that often compounds sleep difficulties in challenging situations. Instead of adding pressure by thinking, "I must get eight perfect hours," focus on "I'm creating the best possible conditions given these circumstances."

I worked with a flight attendant named Sara,h who transformed her approach to sleep across multiple time zones. Rather than fighting her constantly changing schedule, she developed a portable sleep ritual that she could implement anywhere—a specific sequence of stretches, breathing exercises, and relaxation practices that signaled "sleep time" to her brain regardless of what clock or time zone she was in. While she still experienced fatigue from her demanding schedule, this consistent approach helped her body find rest more reliably even as locations and time zones changed.

When It's Time to See a Sleep Specialist

Throughout this chapter, we've explored strategies for managing common sleep struggles. Many sleep issues respond well to self-help approaches, but sometimes, professional guidance becomes necessary. Recognizing when to seek help is an important part of taking your sleep seriously.

Consider consulting a healthcare provider about sleep issues when:

- **You've tried consistent sleep hygiene practices** for several weeks without improvement
- **Daytime sleepiness interferes with your daily functioning**, relationships, or safety
- **Your bed partner reports concerning behaviors** during sleep (gasping, long pauses in breathing, unusual movements)
- **You experience unusual symptoms** like leg sensations that prevent sleep, acting out dreams physically, or excessive daytime sleepiness despite adequate time in bed.

- **Sleep problems occur alongside other health changes** or persist after stressful life circumstances resolve.
- **You're relying on sleep aids** (prescription, over-the-counter, or alcohol) on a regular basis.s
- **Pain constantly disrupts your sleep** despite comfort measures
- **Your sleep schedule is completely misaligned** with your desired or required wake times

Several different professionals can play a role in resolving sleep problems. Your first stop is often your primary care physician, who can review any general health factors that might be disturbing your rest and, when necessary, refer you to more specialized providers. One common referral is to a board-certified sleep specialist—usually a pulmonologist or neurologist who has completed extra training in sleep medicine—who can diagnose and treat complex disorders such as sleep apnea or narcolepsy. Mental-health clinicians also matter: psychologists, psychiatrists, and licensed counselors help when anxiety, depression, or trauma is fueling insomnia, while sleep psychologists with Cognitive Behavioral Therapy for Insomnia (CBT-I) credentials focus on changing the thoughts and habits that keep you awake. For breathing-related issues, an ear-nose-and-throat (ENT) physician can evaluate structural obstructions, and some dentists who practice sleep medicine can fit oral appliances that reduce snoring and treat mild sleep apnea.

Whichever path you take, arrive prepared. Keep a two-week sleep diary that logs when you go to bed and wake up, how long it takes to fall asleep, how many times you're up during the night (and for how long), how rested you feel in the morning, your daytime sleepiness level, and anything that seems to make your sleep better or worse. Sharing this written snapshot helps your clinician spot patterns you might miss and guides the next steps toward healthier, more restorative sleep.

Patience and Persistence: The Path to Better Sleep

As we close this chapter on overcoming sleep struggles, I want to share a perspective that has helped many people I've worked with over the years: Improving disrupted sleep is rarely an overnight process. It's more like tending a garden—consistent care over time yields gradually improving results.

Many people give up on sleep improvements too soon, trying a strategy for a night or two and then abandoning it when they don't see immediate results. But your sleep patterns developed over the years, and meaningful change often requires weeks of consistent practice. The brain needs time to establish new associations and patterns around sleep.

Remember Rachel from the beginning of this chapter, whose racing thoughts kept her awake night after night? Her transformation didn't happen overnight. She committed to her new approaches for three full weeks before the changes really took hold. There were ups and downs along the way—some nights better than others—but the overall trajectory was toward improvement because she gave the process time to work.

This patience applies to all the strategies we've discussed, whether you're managing pain, adjusting to shift work, adapting to CPAP therapy, or calming an anxious mind. Each night is not a pass/fail test but rather one data point in a longer journey toward better rest.

The good news is this trip is worthwhile. Few changes impact your quality of life as profoundly as improving your sleep. Energy, mood, cognitive function, physical health, and relationships—all benefit when you finally overcome the sleep struggles that have held you back.

In our next chapter, we'll explore the often-overlooked spiritual dimension of rest—how faith, mindfulness, and deeper peace can transform not just how you sleep but how you live. Because true rest isn't just about physical comfort or good sleep habits—it's about finding peace in body, mind, and spirit. It's about creating the conditions where deep, restorative sleep can flourish naturally rather than being something you struggle to achieve.

No matter which sleep challenges you face—whether it's the racing thoughts that plagued Rachel, the pain that affected Robert, the breathing issues that James overcame with his CPAP, or the shifting schedules that Sarah navigated as a flight attendant—there are pathways to better rest. The journey may not be quick or simple, but with the right strategies, support, and persistence, truly restorative sleep is possible.

Remember that sleep is not a luxury or an indulgence—it's a biological necessity as fundamental as food and water. By addressing your specific sleep challenges with targeted approaches, you're not being self-indulgent; you're honoring your body's basic needs and creating the foundation for health and well-being in every area of your life.

In my years of helping people with sleep issues, I've seen remarkable transformations when people finally address their specific sleep challenges. Energy returns, mood improves, relationships deepen, and a sense of possibility replaces resignation and fatigue. That transformation is available to you, too, regardless of how long you've struggled with sleep or how complex your challenges may seem.

The path to better sleep begins with understanding your specific obstacles, implementing targeted strategies, seeking help when needed, and giving the process time to work. It's a journey worth taking—one that can quite literally change how you experience every waking moment of your life.

Sleep isn't just a biological function—it's one of the most profound acts of trust we engage in daily. When we close our eyes at night, we're surrendering control, letting go of doing, and trusting in the restorative power of rest. That surrender connects us to something deeper than mere sleep techniques or mattress choices. It connects us to our fundamental need for peace, trust, and renewal—needs that resonate not just in our bodies but in our souls.

Conclusion

Final Thoughts on Rest
As a Lifestyle

THROUGHOUT THIS BOOK, we've explored sleep from many angles—the science behind it, the environment that supports it, the habits that enhance it, the obstacles that prevent it, and even the spiritual dimensions that deepen it. We've covered a lot of ground, from mattress materials to mindfulness practices, from bedroom design to breathing techniques.

But perhaps the most important insight isn't about particular products or practices. It's about perspective—seeing sleep not as an isolated health habit but as an integral part of a well-lived life. When we truly understand this, sleep moves from the periphery of our attention to a central place in our self-care.

The beauty of this approach is its sustainability. While sleep trends and products will come and go, the fundamental principles we've explored remain constant:

- Your body is designed for rhythms of activity and rest
- Your sleep environment significantly influences your sleep quality
- Your daily habits shape your nightly rest
- Your mindset about sleep affects how well you sleep
- Your sleep needs will evolve throughout your life
- Your commitment to quality rest pays dividends in every area of your life

By grounding your sleep practice in these principles rather than in particular products or techniques, you create a flexible, resilient approach that can adapt to your changing needs and circumstances while continuing to support truly restorative rest.

As we close, let me offer some simple next steps to begin or continue your journey toward better sleep. Rather than trying to implement everything at once, consider choosing just one or two of these actions to focus on initially:

1. **Assess your current sleep situation** using the check-in questions we discussed. What's working well? What needs attention?
2. **Evaluate your mattress** for signs that it's still providing the support and comfort you need. If it's not, begin researching options that would better suit your specific sleep needs.

3. **Make one improvement to your sleep environment** this week—perhaps darkening your room more completely, adjusting the temperature, or removing electronic devices.

4. **Establish consistent bedtimes and wake times,** even on weekends, allowing your body's internal clock to stabilize.

5. **Create a simple wind-down ritual** that helps signal to your body and mind that it's time to transition from activity to rest.

6. **Practice one relaxation technique** regularly before bed, whether it's deep breathing, progressive muscle relaxation, or a brief meditation.

7. **Share your sleep goals** with someone who can provide support and gentle accountability.

8. **Track your sleep** for two weeks using whatever method feels manageable, looking for patterns that might guide your next adjustments.

9. **Reflect on your relationship with rest** and how it might be shaped by cultural messages, family patterns, or personal beliefs.

10. **Celebrate small improvements** rather than expecting perfect sleep immediately, recognizing that sustainable change happens gradually.

Remember that sleep improvement is rarely linear. There will be better nights and worse nights, steps forward and occasional steps back. What matters is the overall trajectory—moving gradually but consistently toward sleep that truly restores your body, mind, and spirit.

If you've read this far, you clearly care about improving your sleep and recognize its importance in your life. That awareness itself is a powerful first step. Many people spend years or even decades accepting poor sleep as inevitable, never realizing how much power they have to transform their rest and, by extension, their waking lives.

You've already moved beyond that passive acceptance by educating yourself about sleep and exploring pathways to improvement. That's something to be genuinely proud of. Whether you're just beginning your journey toward better sleep or continuing a path you've already started, know that each step matters—each small change, each mindful choice, each night where you honor your need for rest.

The path to truly restorative sleep isn't always straightforward, and there may be challenges along the way. But I can tell you from both personal experience and from witnessing countless transformations like Tom and Linda's: the journey is worth it. Few things affect your quality of life more than your sleep quality.

So here's to your sleep journey—to nights of deep, peaceful rest and days filled with the energy, clarity, and joy that such rest makes possible. Here's to a life where rest and activity exist in harmonious balance, each supporting and enhancing the other. Here's to the discovery that when we learn to rest well, we also learn to live well.

Sleep tight, my friend. Your best rest—and your best life—awaits.

www.ingramcontent.com/pod-product-compliance
Lightning Source LLC
Chambersburg PA
CBHW021931190326
41519CB00009B/989